THE **POWER** OF **CONFERENCES**

Stories of serendipity, innovation and driving social change

THE **POWER** OF
CONFERENCES

Stories of serendipity, innovation and driving social change

Deborah **EDWARDS** Carmel **FOLEY** Cheryl **MALONE**

UTS
ePRESS

UTS ePRESS
University of Technology Sydney
Broadway NSW 2007
AUSTRALIA
epress.lib.uts.edu.au

Aboriginal and Torres Strait Islander people should be aware that this publication
may contain images or names of deceased persons.

First Published 2017
© 2017 in the text, Deborah Edwards, Carmel Foley and Cheryl Malone
© 2017 in the design, UTS ePRESS

Publication Details

DOI citation: https://doi.org/10.5130/978-0-6481242-0-7

ISBN: 978-0-6481242-0-7 (eBook: PDF)
ISBN: 978-0-6481242-1-4 (paperback)

A catalogue record for this
book is available from the
National Library of Australia

DECLARATION OF CONFLICTING INTEREST The author(s) declare no
potential conflicts of interest with respect to the research, authorship, and/or
publication of this book.

FUNDING The author(s) received financial support from Business Events Sydney
for the research and publication of this book.

UTS ePRESS
Manager: Scott Abbott
Book Editor: Margaret Malone
Cover Design: Cate Furey
Internal Design: Emily Gregory
Enquiries: utsepress@uts.edu.au

For enquiries about third party copyright material reproduced in this work, please
contact UTS ePRESS.

OPEN ACCESS

UTS ePRESS publishes peer reviewed books, journals and conference proceedings
and is the leading publisher of peer reviewed open access journals in Australasia.
All UTS ePRESS online content is free to access and read.

UTS
ePRESS

Acknowledgements

This book was supported and co-funded by Business Events Sydney, and the authors are very appreciative of their assistance and contribution. In particular, sincere thanks go to CEO Lyn Lewis-Smith and Inga Davison, Research and Insights Manager. Special acknowledgement goes to Eve Caroll-Dwyer and Anja Hergesell for their support and contribution during various stages of the project. Finally, we owe an enormous debt of gratitude to Margaret Malone who expertly guided us in the editing of the book.

Foreword

Business Events Sydney's long research partnership with the University of Technology Sydney has shown that conferences deliver knowledge, innovation and best practice. However, the full legacy of an international conference can often only be measured years after that event has taken place.

There will always be a short-term boost to the visitor economy of the host city, but it's often the longer term (or 'long tail') benefits, beyond tourism, that increase the overall value of the event long after it has finished. That's because research shared, innovations explored and connections made are often just the initial catalyst for breakthroughs and global collaborations that come to fruition years later. That was the case for the individuals profiled in this book, for whom conferences have played a seminal role in the development and evolution of their achievements.

When Business Events Sydney partners with organisations bidding to bring their international event to Sydney, we ask what their long-term ambition is. What does success look like for their organisation 5–10 years down the line?

Having that clear vision of how a conference can help to achieve a wider objective is invaluable and provides a framework with which to measure the impact on a much wider scale than just delegate numbers or direct expenditure.

Yet, sometimes the most important and exciting legacies come from unexpected encounters – the ones that lead to unlikely collaborations or opportunities to take research from one field and apply it to a totally different area.

At other times genuine progress is made simply by bringing people with a common cause together and uniting them behind a clear and compelling purpose; whether to accelerate a cure for disease, raise money for a particular cause, or secure greater profile and support for a campaign to create real and lasting social change.

With the internet providing a wealth of information at people's fingertips and bringing communities together remotely, and technology constantly advancing research capabilities, we are often asked "Will conferences ever become obsolete?" The experts in this book unanimously agree that there is still no substitute for the power of congregation. They believe conferences have a bright future, and so do we.

Whether you organise, attend or support conferences, we hope this book and these stories will inspire you to think big and give you the courage and passion to use these events to help drive social change and create a lasting legacy.

Lyn Lewis-Smith
CEO, Business Events Sydney

BUSINESS EVENTS
SYDNEY

Contents

Introduction

A chance encounter at a conference sets up a series of unfolding events. In 1982, immunologist Ian Frazer attended his first international gastroenterology conference in Canberra, Australia. After his presentation on genital warts, a colleague, Dr Gabrielle Medley, discussed with him the potential link between the human papillomavirus and cancer. This meeting proved fateful, as it helped to put him on the path that would ultimately lead to the development of the HPV vaccine. This vaccine is now used across the globe, and may eradicate cervical cancer within a generation.

This book seeks to explore and understand these long-term outcomes: what we loosely refer to as the 'long tail' of conference impact. By doing so, we hope to add to an increasingly complex picture of the value of conferences. For, despite the costs and effort involved in hosting and attending conferences, despite all the online communication options for the circulation of knowledge and commentary, many thousands of events, involving many thousands of people coming together, take place around the world each year. What makes them so worthwhile? How can we plan and design conferences to allow for the full range of potential benefits and outcomes?

For the purpose of this book, a conference is defined as a formal meeting in which many people gather in order to talk about ideas or problems related to a particular topic, academic discipline or industry area. For example, the conferences referred to in the following case studies include (inter alia) medical, engineering, science and education conferences. Conferences may also be referred to as congresses, symposiums, meetings and business events; however, throughout this book we will use the term conferences.

Conference attendees usually include a mix of academics (including postgraduate students) and industry professionals, with occasional community involvement; for example, patients, carers and advocates sometimes attend medical conferences. Many conferences also feature exhibitors who may have a business or research stake in the topic area of the conference.

Most conferences are linked to a national or international professional association. Some are held in the same destination each year. However, others, like the International AIDS Conference run by the International AIDS Society, move around to different destinations, often raising global awareness of sector-related issues. Some are carefully designed to leverage particular outcomes linked to the mission of the association(s) organising the event. Others are run on a more ad hoc basis, without specific objectives other than to provide a meeting point for attendees who each have their own related but distinct agendas. Conference outcomes, then, can range from the planned to the serendipitous; from the tangible to the intangible.

Typically, conferences are evaluated in terms of their short-term impact, both individually and collectively. Individually, most conferences have some level of post-event evaluation and this is often focused around delegate satisfaction with various aspects of the event (such as venue, program, speakers). Collectively, conferences are evaluated by governments and industry, mostly in terms of their financial contribution by way of visitor expenditure. Governments are aware of the significant influx of new money that can result from hosting an international or domestic conference, and cities around the world compete to be the preferred destination site for conferences. However, there is a growing recognition that the value of conferences extends well beyond tourism and should not be measured merely by direct financial contribution (Dwyer, Mellor, Mistilis & Mules 2000).

In this book, we argue that new money, attractive as it is, is just one of the contributions that a conference can make to individuals, industry, government agencies and the wider destination community. The primary audience for this book are those who work in the conference industry, educators and students who will go on to work in this field.

Rethinking The Value Of Conferences

A number of studies have pointed to a lack of recognition of the full value of conferences in traditional evaluations (Carlsen, Getz & Soutar 2001; Wood 2009; Foley, Edwards, Schlenker & Lewis-Smith 2013). As such, there is a clear need to consider conferences in more sophisticated ways that take us beyond traditional short-term economic impact measures (Pickernell, O'Sullivan, Senyard & Keast 2007). Evaluating conferences without taking account of the wider and longer term benefits seriously underestimates their value to all stakeholders.

Previous research (Jago & Deery 2010; Teulan 2010) has identified a number of opportunities that conferences can provide, including knowledge expansion, community outcomes, innovative and collaborative projects, international relations, trade and networking opportunities, education, and enhanced business-to-business relationships. Similarly, industry reports (such as those produced by The Business Events Industry Strategy Group 2008), which have offered evidence-based examples of the economic benefits that conferences can bring, have also noted their potential to 'promote and showcase Australian expertise and innovation to the world and attract global leaders and investment decision makers ... to Australia'.

A peer-reviewed academic Australian study sought to examine the broader legacies of conferences (Foley, Edwards, Schlenker & Lewis-Smith 2013; Foley, Schlenker & Edwards 2010). Drawing on a range of conferences from across industry sectors, the authors collected data using in-depth interviews and secondary data analysis (Edwards, Foley & Schlenker 2011; Foley, Edwards & Hergesell, 2016; Foley, Edwards, Hergesell & Schlenker 2014; Foley, Edwards & Schlenker, 2014; Foley, Schlenker & Edwards 2010; Foley, Schlenker, Edwards & Lewis-Smith 2013). Through the analysis, six core themes emerged, reflecting the benefits and outcomes that can arise from conferences: (a) knowledge expansion, (b) networking, (c) relationships and collaboration, (d) fundraising and future research capacity, (e) raising awareness and profiling, and (f) showcasing and destination reputation.

Within these core themes, it was argued that there were more than 45 possible benefits, tangible and intangible, including the exchange of ideas, building of professional reputation, and strengthening of relationship bonds and resource ties. Application of new techniques and technologies, improved skills, and relocation to the conference destination to live and work were among the tangible benefits.

Through this and subsequent research, our studies identified a 'long tail' effect (Edwards, Foley & Schlenker 2011): participants reported that not only were the benefits and outcomes felt during the conference or within 12 months following the conference, they were also experiencing the benefits three to five years after the conference. Some added that the benefits and outcomes were still to be realised. These findings suggested to us that more needed to be known about the benefits and outcomes that occurred well after the conference had finished and that we needed to understand the quality of the impact, to understand the full value of conferences.

The idea of the long tail was popularised by Chris Anderson (2004) to explain an anomaly in the music industry. He noticed that infinite shelf space in the form of the internet, combined with real-time information, led to sales that collectively grew to become a large share of total sales (Brynjolfsson, Hu & Simester 2011). Such was its importance that Zhu, Song, Ni, Ren and Li (2016) suggested that the long tail was itself a new market.

According to Anderson (2004), the long tail describes a frequency distribution pattern in which the number of events in the tail is greater than the number of events in the immediate high-frequency area.

In the context of our research on conference impact and evaluation, the idea of the long tail presented us with a novel way to conceptualise and capture those outcomes that come to fruition years, and even decades, after the event has taken place. We asked ourselves: how can we measure the long tail? This was a slippery problem, and after much consideration we realised that a qualitative approach to data collection was going to be more meaningful than a quantifiable measurement approach.

Conferences: Providing 'Out Of The Ordinary' Experiences

The treadmill of daily existence in contemporary societies has been identified as a less than ideal environment for forming meaningful relationships, sharing knowledge or stopping to think with the people around us (McDonald, Wearing & Ponting 2008). Busy people often find it difficult to let go of their 'to do' lists for the sake of spending time with companions (Foley 2017). However, in order for meaningful social interactions to occur, 'out of the ordinary' opportunities are needed to encourage people to take time out from their busy schedules and established routines.

A conference is one such 'out of the ordinary' experience that gives attendees a break from everyday demands and facilitates shared social contexts (Small, Harris, Wilson & Ateljevic 2011) which are conducive to knowledge sharing. Such experiences provide opportunities for delegates to become part of a network of lifelong professional and personal friends – a network which can increase exponentially over time (Hickson 2006); they provide a temporal context for intensified knowledge exchange and social interaction (Maskell, Bathelt & Malmberg 2005); and they offer the chance to build relationships with other regular participants, which can result in improved performance (Bahlmann, Huysman, Elfring & Groenewegen 2009).

Conferences also provide unique opportunities to showcase, construct and brainstorm new ideas, strategies and technologies. Face-to-face communication and live presentations at such events can create a special impetus for developing new professional relationships and research collaborations. Bathelt, Malmberg and Maskell (2004) suggest that innovation, knowledge creation and learning are all best understood when seen as the result of interactive processes where people possessing different types of knowledge and competencies come together to exchange information. Such exchanges and interactions can occur in different ways, including via social media or video conferencing, but the camaraderie and sense of community that can develop around conferences, the appeal of engaging face-to-face with peers, and the relationships that are developed and enhanced contribute to both personal and social legacies that other forms of online communication cannot match. In this social context, the sharing of knowledge and creative ideas occurs and common meanings are developed through interactions (Edwards et al. 2011).

Diagram 1 (page 12) was developed as a result of our previous work, where we established that conferences are catalysts for thriving economies, with benefits accruing to individuals and communities immediately and over time. This latest research seeks to expand upon this conceptualisation by dramatically expanding the perceived time frame in which the outcomes of conferences are realised.

To do this we decided to look backwards; to look back at conferences from the end of the long tail. We interviewed a range of people who had realised major achievements in their careers. We asked these people if and how their work had been influenced by conferences. What we explore through the stories in this book are the long tail legacies: the conference outcomes that reach fruition years and even decades after the conference is held. The HPV vaccine mentioned in the Introduction is an example of a long tail legacy. While conference research has established a comprehensive understanding of how legacies are facilitated by conferences over the short term, this book tells long tail stories from the field. We present the roles played by conferences in the diverse careers of influential innovators, researchers and thought leaders from across government, industry and academe in a wide range of fields.

DIAGRAM 1 CONFERENCES –
LONG-TERM CATALYSTS FOR THRIVING ECONOMIES

Source: Foley, Edwards & Hergesell (2016)

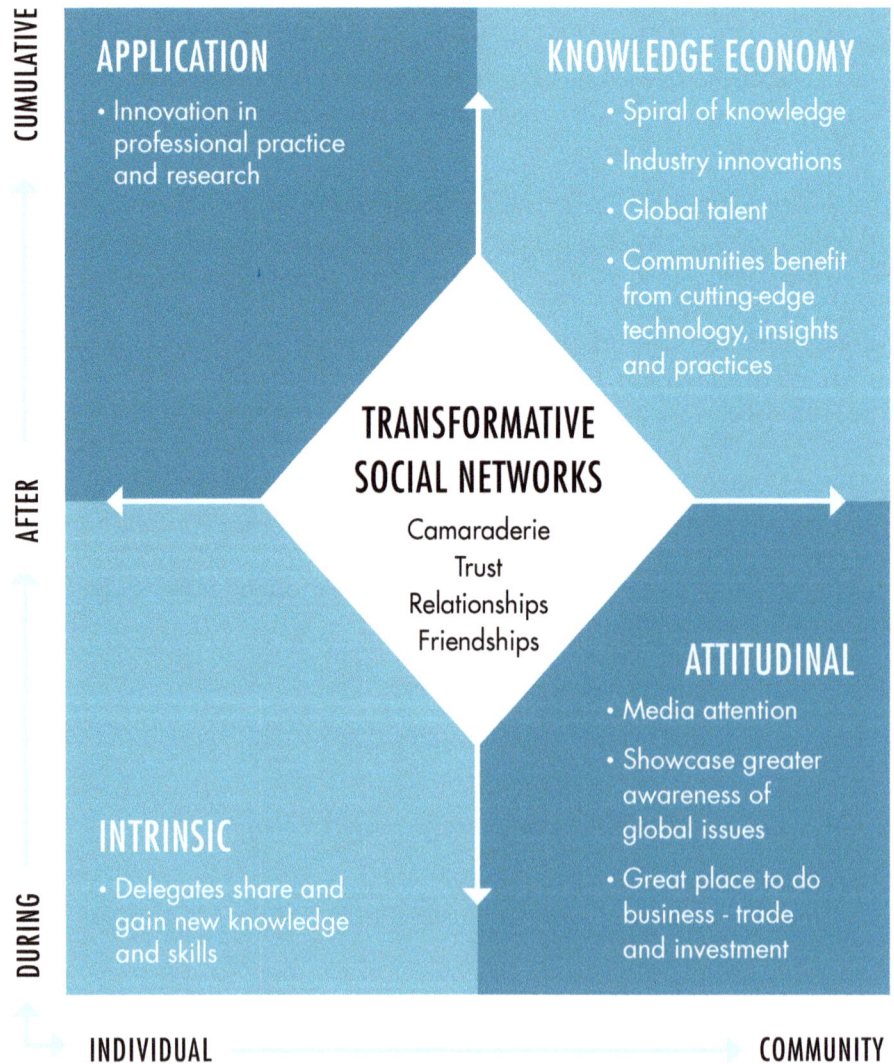

CUMULATIVE

APPLICATION
- Innovation in professional practice and research

KNOWLEDGE ECONOMY
- Spiral of knowledge
- Industry innovations
- Global talent
- Communities benefit from cutting-edge technology, insights and practices

TRANSFORMATIVE SOCIAL NETWORKS
Camaraderie
Trust
Relationships
Friendships

AFTER

ATTITUDINAL
- Media attention
- Showcase greater awareness of global issues
- Great place to do business - trade and investment

INTRINSIC
- Delegates share and gain new knowledge and skills

DURING

INDIVIDUAL — **COMMUNITY**

Collecting The Stories

The stories presented in this book provide clear evidence of the ways in which conferences allow delegates to network, learn and innovate, and to co-create value as they forge new relationships and common agendas. Participants were selected from a diverse range of fields to represent the influence of a broad range of conferences (medicine, physics, applied science, agriculture, social policy). We looked for high achievers in each field (Nobel Prize recipients, industry and community leaders). We chose people who had attended their first conference well before 2007, to ensure a suitably long tail of conference influence for the research for this book (conducted in 2017). A list of potential participants was drawn up and each was contacted by email and phone and asked to participate. Semi-structured interviews were conducted, recorded and transcribed with those who agreed (65 per cent). How to deliver these stories was an issue we needed to consider. If we structured the stories for one type of audience would we alienate another? The stories were so personal that we decided to keep them engaging and accessible.

Further secondary research was conducted to add to each case study. Interested readers will find a bibliography that provides further information and reading at the end of the book. The stories were then returned to participants for verification. A decision was made by the authors to deliver the stories in an informal tone rather than use academic language and style. We wanted these stories and an understanding of the power of conferences to be accessible, not just to academics and their students, but also to government, industry and the broader community. Stories of serendipity, innovation and driving social change are relevant to us all. The stories are presented in no particular order; rather, we invite the reader to start with whichever story is of most interest to them.

THE **STORIES**

THE **STORIES**

01

Mary Bebawy

Understanding How Cancer Cells Communicate

There are few amongst us whose lives have not been touched in some way by the challenge of cancer. In fact, with more and more people projected to live well into their 80s, current estimates are that one in every two (men) or three (women) will develop cancer before they turn 85; a sobering statistic, without doubt. But just as remarkable is that, whilst a diagnosis of cancer 40 years ago was virtually a death sentence, today more than 50 per cent of all cancer patients survive for at least a decade, and for certain types of cancer, survival rates are higher.

Despite these gains, little is understood about cancer recurrence and cancer cell behaviour. However, one Australian woman is helping to change that. For over 20 years, Mary Bebawy has researched the way cancer cells communicate and essentially clone themselves in a fight for survival, in the process unlocking some of the disease's most potent secrets and opening up a whole new field of scientific investigation.

"I've always been interested in cancer research. It's a disease... it's so complex.... There's so much to be done and it affects every family at some time. There's an arsenal of therapeutic drugs available to kill off cancer cells, so why is it that cancer cells tend to reoccur?"

A cell biologist, Bebawy decided to launch her assault on the disease by looking at the mechanisms driving cancer cell survival. She started by examining drug resistance. At that time, it was known that some cells were resistant to drugs and others weren't, but what wasn't clear was why or how the number of resistant cells seemed to be able to increase and hence survive the chemo-therapeutics, as though their resistance was being acquired after they'd been exposed to the drugs.

"We started focussing on multi-drug resistance and it's an area I am committed to because it is the basis of anticancer treatment failure."

In 2009, Mary Bebawy and her team at the University of Sydney found that, whilst certain cells were susceptible (responsive) to cancer drugs, others were resistant – and those resistant cells were programmed to seek out the susceptible cells and transfer their genetic material into drug-sensitive cells, virtually cloning themselves and their resistance into the non-resistant cells. She presented her new ideas at various conferences. It took time for the scientific community to get their heads around her important discovery, as it challenged previous thinking about how and why chemotherapy sometimes failed or patients relapsed, but the research spoke for itself.

A graduate of the University of New South Wales in the mid-90s, Bebawy did her Honours degree in cancer research at St George hospital where she was exposed to expert practitioners, researchers and surgeons. In particular, her supervising professor at the time made sure that his team attended and presented at conferences irrespective of what level they were at.

"To have that exposure as an Honours student where one is in a room with the leading researchers in the field, it builds your confidence and reinforces what you're learning and it's just so important."

These early experiences ignited a passion for the field, and she decided to do her PhD in the Pharmacy faculty at the University of Sydney, looking at mechanisms that were driving cancer cell survival. During her studies, Mary kept asking the same questions:

"If there is an arsenal of therapeutic drugs that are available, why is it that patients start to relapse and why do people die from this disease? Why haven't we cured this disease, why do we relapse? Why do some people survive 20, 30 years with cancer and others pass away in just a few months? And why do some people relapse and others don't?"

And it is in that area of relapse and drug-resistance that Bebawy's discoveries are having the most significant impact. In 2009, she and her team discovered that resistance could be acquired.

"We found they do adapt. Cancer cells transfer survival proteins amongst each other. Essentially the resistant cells shed tiny vesicles packed with functional nucleic acids and proteins which then dock onto the drug-responsive cell and re-template the protein and nucleic acid landscape in the recipient cell to reflect that of the donor cell, making it resistant to the drugs.

"That was our first major finding. We discovered that the cells 'talk' to one another in this way and we were the first to discover that this is how resistance can be disseminated throughout a cancer cell population within

a matter of only a few hours. The area took off from there and we've been publishing prolifically ever since. We are at the international forefront of this area given that we discovered the phenomenon and we're now looking at other cancer traits such as increased metastatic capacity and various other things."

Now an Associate Professor at the University of Technology Sydney (UTS), Bebawy is convinced that what she's learned at conferences throughout her career has been a crucial factor in her development, and sees conferences as opportunities for further education beyond higher education.

"I go to conferences primarily to learn. It's the only way in which I can further my knowledge because it is in these conferences and the works presented there that I hear new things. Many of the conferences I attend require that works not yet be published, and it is here that you are exposed to the very latest technologies, the latest methodologies, latest knowledge etc."

She says that there is no way you can acquire that knowledge via the internet or by sifting through a book.

"You just can't access it because it hasn't been published yet – so you have to go to these conferences to be one step ahead in your thinking and in the development of your thoughts."

Certainly, Bebawy admits, it's possible for knowledge to filter through via other mediums, and for ideas and insights to occur regardless of conference attendance, but she says it's a question of how long it might otherwise have taken and the lives that might have been impacted in the meantime.

"I can't really say whether my ideas and discoveries would have occurred without conferences, because I'm exposed to all sorts of knowledge, but I just really feel that conferences have played a significant part in my learning. Yes, perhaps I could have read it in some paper or something eventually but that may have impacted on the timeliness of things because, as I said before, at conferences you're getting the latest research before publication, and without that initial information from the conference I probably wouldn't have come across that idea or research so quickly."

Equally, some of the greatest benefits from what she hears at conferences can take years to become relevant or realised.

"In research we're hearing things from here, there and everywhere, so it's hard to recall specific examples of things I've actually learned at conferences, but what I do find all the time, is that I can go to a conference one year, and I can hear someone talking about a certain thing (like their methods, or maybe a finding they've looked at in another model), and you don't think that much about it because at the time it might not be all that relevant or important to what you're doing, but then a couple of years later as your research progresses, that moment comes back.

"You think about it. You remember. You can picture where you were. And you go back to the abstract or program from the conference, you read the abstract, you then start looking up that individual's papers to see what else they've done since and that's the way that I have found conferences have really helped me. It's not immediate, it's actually usually a couple of years later – that's where my most important application of that knowledge has come into play because it wasn't immediately recognised as being relevant when I'd heard it before."

Other benefits can also come about years later in terms of collaborations, research findings and invitations.

"Sometimes, years later, you might also be invited to something because someone's heard the extent of your work and what you're doing at a previous conference and they then want you to participate or perhaps to be part of an organising committee for the next conference. This is how collaborations often arise."

Now a highly respected and sought-after PhD supervisor, Bebawy was encouraged by her supervisor at St George hospital to attend conferences, and now insists her own students do the same.

"I travelled to Adelaide for my first ever conference and had to give a short presentation, which was quite intimidating, but to have that exposure and to be in that forum where you've got top people sitting there builds your confidence and reinforces what you're learning and I just think it's so

important. I make sure now that when I travel, my students are with me. With my current teaching load I can only really attend about 2 conferences a year, but I usually go to them with an entourage of students."

So convinced of their value, Bebawy's students attend conferences both nationally and internationally, and if not on scholarships, Bebawy often funds students from her own research budget.

One of the most important ideals she tries to convey to her students is the need to read and learn outside their own area of interest and to attend what they think might be unrelated seminars.

"Research is dynamic, and it changes depending on what you're finding at the time, and it could be that you're finding something so new that no-one's really looked at it in the field, and as a result you need to look elsewhere. This is a great way for collaborations to arise."

Bebawy recently developed one such important collaboration in the area of tissue bio-mechanics after listening to a physics researcher from Perth talk about a new technique he was using.

"I was in the audience and I spoke to Prof Vincent Wallace very briefly afterwards and then about a year later he came to Sydney and literally was knocking on my door wanting to explore what we had spoken about. I sent a student over to him mid last year, and he brought people into the project from London, and an electrical engineer, and we've got a publication coming out soon and are applying for further funding together. This is an example of how you can meet an individual in a scientific forum and there's a domino effect, you know, you co-supervise a student, you publish a paper, you bring in other international researchers in the field and great outcomes such as grants and publications result."

Mary says that apart from the insights academics and researchers can gain at conferences, clinicians, too, can glean important first-hand knowledge that can be used to help their own patients more efficiently.

"Industry is always strongly represented, and clinicians working with patients are there ... Those sort of people can also then be exposed to new ideas that have not yet been published, and which contribute to disease

state management in the long term."

According to Bebawy, it is the act of physically engaging with the conference environment that helps stimulate higher thought and generate new ideas. She says she is not a fan of the recent push towards use of webinars, believing participants need to be actively present at a conference to get the real benefits.

"You need to dissociate from your usual environment and allow yourself to be positioned in the conference environment; allowing yourself to be physically present."

"Conferences can go for three or four days and you need to get away; otherwise, there's no way you can actually absorb and ... recall what it is you've listened to down the track."

She believes the use of webinars and teleconferencing at conferences is at times akin to other shallow approaches to learning, such as listening to lectures at home rather than sitting in a lecture theatre with the expert.

"You've got a deep approach to learning and a shallow approach to learning, and with a shallow approach you're skimming the surface. The possibility of recall then is significantly compromised, whereas with a deeper approach to learning – when you're sitting there with the speaker and you engage with the speakers – you immerse yourself and the learning is personal. You're engaging with the content and the speakers; with whomever it is you want to talk to ... and it's only then that important concepts are reinforced; in that deeper learning."

She maintains that, although you can still learn from reading and researching, recall of that information is slower and more difficult.

"I'm a visual learner, and when there is physical engagement and visual cues like those associated with actually attending a conference, you can remember things more easily and recall relevant information more quickly."

Similarly, she says that some of the best conferences pay attention to creating environments where attendees can casually speak to people, for example, at conference dinners or informal events.

As far as shaping the level of public engagement and discussion on scientific issues goes, Mary feels public forums are a great way to get important findings and advances into the public sphere.

"Members of the general public aren't usually present at conferences, but I've participated in public forums that were open to the general public that had media present, and when people have picked up on things and said 'Wow... what is this research?', the media have become involved and the messages start to get out. The Sydney Morning Herald has done a few stories on our work, so at public forums or larger conferences with the media present there is the potential for public discussion to be influenced."

Another consideration in terms of the importance of conferences to Mary's progress is the role they play in helping her obtain ongoing funding. In 2009 the Cancer Council supported Mary's research by way of a $120 000 per year grant over three years, and since then their projects have attracted other funding, thanks largely to the contribution they've made to this area of research, and because of their willingness to share their achievements with others at conferences and public forums.

"This is all an important part of international recognition and contribution to the field.

Their work has recently gone translational, which is where basic scientific findings and laboratory experiments are 'translated' firstly into clinical trials.

"We've just published an article in NEOPLASIA showing how we can monitor the number of these vesicles being shed in multiple myeloma patients and then link those levels to how patients are handling or responding to chemotherapy. There were times we could pick up patient relapse weeks in advance of ... traditional tests – so it's a hot area and yes, it's very exciting."

Finally, on a scale of 1 to 10 in terms of the importance of conferences to knowledge creation and diffusion and the flow of important information, Mary has no hesitation in ranking conferences a clear 10.

"Conferences are essential on many levels and they help show you're engaged with the scientific community and that your research is significant and topical. We're getting recognised at conferences and we're getting invitations from top conferences now, which is a huge privilege."

But those most truly privileged are the thousands of scientists, researchers and practitioners being exposed to Mary and her team's findings at such conferences, and the millions whose lives or those of loved ones may be saved as a result of her dogged determination to unlock the secrets of this disease.

THE STORIES

02

Pia Winberg

Venus Shell Systems,
A Marine Biomass Farm

Ask most people what they think of seaweed, and they are likely to mention sushi. But one Australian woman has spent the past decade trying to expand perceptions of this aquatic plant, which she believes is one of the stars of sustainable food sources for the future.

Dr Pia Winberg, who graduated from the University of Wollongong (UOW) with a Doctorate in Marine Conservation Ecology in 2008, believes Australia's extensive coastline and good, clean waters make commercial production of seaweed in Australia not only viable but a highly profitable and socially ethical venture, particularly as the world searches for strategies to tackle increasing food demands and decreasing supplies of wild (ocean) fish. According to Dr Winberg:

"Cultivation of seaweed in the Asian countries is huge, with a global crop worth over AUD$6 billion – and that's just the crop itself. But Australia and the West are hardly cultivating it at all. Europe is starting to show some interest, and France in particular is developing in the area, but Australia has done very little."

That $6 billion crop equates to about 8 million tonnes of wet seaweed each year. Wild harvesting (predominantly from the Atlantic Ocean) accounts for only 5 per cent of this. Demand far exceeds the rate at which wild beds can regrow, hence 95 per cent of the total crop is grown and harvested in established 'farms' found mainly in China, Korea, Japan and the Philippines.

Despite seaweed not being part of a 'traditional' Australian diet, Australia imports about $17 million worth annually, and over recent years demand has been steadily increasing by an impressive 30 per cent each year. Whilst its place in Asian cuisine is well known, what is less known is how widely it is used in other areas, such as improving soil quality and plant health in agriculture, as a cleansing/purifying agent in soaps, toothpastes and skin products, and for its amazing health and medicinal benefits including anti-cancer, anti-oxidant, anti-inflammatory and anti-viral capacities. In fact, with its high levels of omega-3 fatty acids, calcium, minerals and iodine, along with the ease with which it is grown and harvested, it is fast gaining a reputation as one of nature's super foods.

So confident was Winberg in the potential of this superfood that in 2014, with the help of motivated investors, she made the bold decision to move away from full-time academia to establish a pilot seaweed production facility, Venus Shell Systems, near Nowra. The first of its kind in the country, the project has since proven itself to be scalable, technically viable and capable of producing good yields. Although there are still hurdles to overcome in terms of accessing markets, it seems Venus Shell Systems is on track to become a player in the global seaweed production industry.

However, getting the support of government, community and business for her ideas hasn't been easy and, according to this 'scientist come entrepreneur', one of the most powerful tools she has utilised has been conferences: to gather information, make important contacts, and get her messages heard by those who needed to listen.

"The conferences I've attended over the last 10 years have actually been very, very, important in terms of me garnering confidence, developing a broad base of knowledge, and helping me to interact with relevant people in my field. And that's helped me to now become internationally recognised as someone with expertise in this field of research."

Early in her academic career, Winberg recognised that for science to be truly valued it needed to be made relevant to the wider community, and for her that meant finding ways to translate what was learned in the lab into practical outcomes that could make a difference to people's lives.

"Scientists just tend to publish in peer reviewed journals and it's very hard to get the ideas communicated well through mainstream media because we're scientists, and that's not the traditional way it's done. I always felt the missing link was finding ways to make [scientific] conversations really relevant to human society. I wanted to know what other people were thinking, and I found that going to a range of different conferences was a really important means of broadening my perspectives on what was important to people; what they were doing, where they're headed, and what the community's overall trajectory was."

After attending her first conference in 2005, Winberg was approached by the Rural Industries Research and Development Corporation (AgriFutures

Australia), which funded a study to identify ways in which her research could be applied commercially for new seaweed crops in Australia. Soon after, they funded her attendance at the 2008 International Society for Applied Phycology conference in Ireland to enable her to gain knowledge about what was happening in the field internationally and to learn about how such industries could be established and developed in Australia.

"As part of that funding I was to bring back a detailed report for general publication, so I sat there and absorbed all I could about what was clearly a very broad and diverse field. Everything from biofuel production to food growing to harvesting and all sorts of different aspects I otherwise wouldn't have ever even thought to spend time reading about."

After graduating in 2008, she stayed on at UOW and, alongside her teaching and supervisory roles, established the university's Shoalhaven Marine and Freshwater Centre (SMFC). As Director of the centre, she and her students began researching ways marine ecosystems could be enhanced by the introduction of seaweed, as well as investigating sustainable marine food production systems. In particular, they became interested in ways that seaweed could be commercially and mass produced for large-scale human and animal consumption through the practice of aquaculture. Sensing this was a potential growth area of the future, she threw herself into learning all she could about the industry, and insists that going to conferences was the most useful element in that process, both for herself and for her students.

"You understand a lot more from a conference than you do from sitting, reading very specific information in peer reviewed literature, so I spent a lot of time going to conferences and interacting and networking with economists, investors and business people outside my field of research.

"I also made sure my students attended as many conferences as possible because they're very good training for them; scary – but really important. As a research student you always feel overwhelmed in your first few conferences because you don't understand the hierarchical structure inside academia but they're always so valuable. I think even undergraduates should be really strongly encouraged and supported to go to conferences in those early years of their education so they learn how information

is disseminated and then they learn more quickly how to contribute constructively and confidently to the conversations as their careers develop."

After the 2008 conference she went to as many others as she could, always learning but also presenting her own material, and then in 2014, with the help of Rural Industries and some very supportive Sydney-based businesses, she coordinated her own International Phycology conference in Australia.

That conference was highly successful, particularly in terms of Winberg's philosophy of making science relevant to the wider community.

"We really wanted to make this conference relevant to the public in some way. We wanted to have all the important delegates and information there but we also wanted to communicate things in a fun way because the public [aren't] going to sit there and listen to boring professor presentations."

So, as part of that focus, and with Australia's growing reputation for diverse cuisine and food innovation, they decided to put together a recipe book based on seaweed.

"We brought 27 seaweeds from around the world – from researchers in industry that were actually delegates at the conference, and gave those seaweeds to 18 local food chefs, and said, 'Cook anything but sushi!'.

"We thought this was a great way to not only showcase Australia's culinary expertise to the international delegates, but also to make the international delegates more relevant to the locals. We launched the book, Coastal Chef, right there at the conference, and so automatically those scientists coming from as far away as Portugal or northern Canada had already collaborated and were now partners in a book production with local chefs when they arrived at the door.

"At the opening event we had attendees from the public – just mainstream people interested in food – as well as the chefs and the delegates, and the dishes were served to everyone. We generated a lot of media and public interest, and everyone had a lot of fun, so I think that was an important strategy."

The conference also included an open public debate with well-known media personality and comedian, Adam Spencer, as MC to draw in a crowd beyond academics and to put the controversial topic of algae and biofuels on the table.

"I believe the public has an interest in understanding more about this whole area of sustainability and biofuels etc. so we put together a panel of six scientific experts as well as local energy and sustainability professionals and had a debate with a poll going in and out from the public's perception.

"It was really useful and a bit of reality check to find out what the public thinks and what they think the challenges are because scientists can get so caught up in tiny details of research that they sometimes just forget the relevance of the big picture."

Winberg saw this element of the conference as being very powerful because of how it managed to influence how people felt about future prospects for algae and solutions to sustainable biofuels.

"It was very important. When we did the polling we realised we had actually shifted the audience's perceptions of algae for biofuels before and after the event, which was great."

But Winberg does admit the time and effort spent coordinating the event was significant.

"It's a lot of hard work and personal risk. So much time is spent in organising all the details, and whilst conferences are clearly recognised as being important, you're not very well supported or well rewarded inside universities when you make the effort to host one. That's why, sadly, there are a lot of academics who never make that effort.

"It's a shame, really, because the whole experience was very positive and very rewarding, and although I'm outside the university arena now, I still feel so much more could be achieved if academics were encouraged, supported and rewarded for hosting more conferences in their fields."

What she found most valuable at many of the conferences she attended throughout the years was the opportunity to consider a wide range of relevant perspectives.

"You really can't grasp the emotional aspects of an issue from reading black and white scientific articles because the culture of communication is very restricted; very factual.

"At many of these conferences it was exactly the opposite – and there were some very heated, controversial questions and debates. I hadn't been aware of many of these controversies or the level of antagonism there was across some sectors, so it gave me an insight into differences of opinion and what those opinions were based upon. Over time it also gave me the confidence to participate at that level and put ideas forward because unless you're exposed to those opinions and those debates in a conference forum you can't understand the whole picture."

Another conference strategy Winberg adopted was to cross-pollinate her ideas across a range of conference types. Rather than just attending seaweed or aquaculture events which gave her the latest information in her own field, she also targeted events that were only marginally relevant (such as the psychology, nutrition and aquaculture conferences and Biomarine Business Convention), using each opportunity to learn, but also to get her message out.

"It's so important to go out of your own area of research and step out of your comfort zone.

"Sometimes, you go to those algae conferences, and you're just saying, 'Well, my algae is better than your algae' and it doesn't actually take you anywhere whereas, if you go to, say, a nutrition conference, and you say, for example, 'Well, how about putting seaweed into one of your clinical trial projects and seeing how seaweeds can contribute to very important chronic diseases or malnutrition?' you can really take your area of expertise and jump into another area of research and put it into relevance for that area.

"That's where innovation happens; with a cross-fertilization of ideas.

"It's very hard to start publishing in a totally new field of research that you don't have a track record of publishing in or have much knowledge in, but you can go to a conference and present what you know and interact with people who have other areas of expertise and create new projects."

Winberg says that, even though you may be relegated to a small, short session, or there may only be a few attendees in your session, you can still have a big impact on people's thinking.

"When you bring your ideas to a range of conferences you can have that information disseminated and discussed and tweaked and refined before you've actually, you know, finished and delivered your findings on a $200,000 research grant, for example.

"You can bring your ideas 'to the table', in a sense, and many of the research projects and collaborations I've received funding for have been based on meeting people this way at different types of conferences."

One such important collaboration was with nutritionist Professor Barbara Meyer. Despite the fact that both researchers were based at the University of Wollongong, they had never met, and only after speaking at a conference did they realise the potential there was to work together.

"I went to a conference on seafood and health, and while I was there I met a nutritionist from my own university who started talking to me about an interesting study on reducing aggression that had been done in a UK prison by feeding inmates omega-3s.

"I told her about a new prison in our region, and talked about my seaweed research and we thought we'd try to replicate that study here in an Australian prison, and so we did, and our findings were later published in a very high-level peer review journal.

"The project was also featured on Catalyst last year on the ABC, and now we're continuing to collaborate on a range of health and nutrition projects and have a whole host of undergraduate students taking our knowledge on seaweeds and seaweed biomass and putting it into clinical trials."

With researchers and students from other health-related areas becoming excited about the projects and joining the team, they are now in the process of establishing a formalised program of research and, according to Winberg, the whole thing was triggered as a direct result of conferences.

She said conferences have been integral in enabling her to engage other researchers, industry, government regulators and the community in the questions and issues she saw as being important. Those that specifically bring in business and researchers from industry, establishing a combined focus on innovation, progress and funding, realise some of the best outcomes. This is because they set up very specific partnering schedules and programs during the conference.

"There are some big silos in government research areas versus the regulatory areas and they don't cross-seminate ideas easily, so I spent [a] lot of time linking and talking to people in all of those sectors to get a broader perspective on top of things I simply read about."

One perspective that was shaped through interaction at conferences was the way in which science, and specifically some of the conservation initiatives being proposed or implemented, could potentially impact local people.

"In regional communities where things like fishing are very important you need to understand that sure, you can stop fishing to protect the fish – but then you end up with high unemployment. Then, high unemployment leads to other negative social issues so you have to look at the transition of industries and how to address the broader economic and social impacts of conservation; how do you make the two work together?"

Frustrated by policy-makers' reluctance to make important changes or even acknowledge the validity of research findings of climate scientists, Winberg admits she has walked a courageous path somewhere between private enterprise and academia for most of her career, having always as a priority the enhancement of marine eco-systems in ways that were not only sustainable but also able to improve our way of life.

As a result of these experiences, Winberg has no hesitation rating conferences a clear "ten out of ten" in terms of their importance to knowledge diffusion in her field, and says their role in helping her attract funding throughout her career was crucial.

"They really are just so important on so many levels, particularly as part of a long-term strategy for getting public funding. At the conferences you become aware of what sources there are and they become aware of you.

"I realised early on that the FRDC (Fisheries Research and Development Corporation) was a major government funding body for aquaculture research but I don't think they'd taken seaweed seriously as a contender for future aquaculture or research and development projects until they kept hearing me speaking about it at conferences. You just have to keep flying the flag for your area of research and why it's relevant and slowly but surely with a track record of persistence, you can demonstrate why your area warrants more investment."

The strategy seems to be working for Winberg, who last year was one of only 10 people invited by the FRDC to attend an important funding and strategies meeting about the future of aquaculture in Australia.

"That's happened purely because of attending conferences and introducing my ideas to these people."

Winberg also stressed how important conferences were for making international contacts that often translate into working collaborations.

"Through conferences, I have an international network of professional friends, and we catch up at other conferences or when we're visiting each other's country. We know that even if there's not an immediate opportunity for close collaboration, we keep a friendship sort of relationship going because we know that probably in a year or two there's going to be a real time and place to work together. They're like sitting in your head and you might suddenly go, 'Ah, this person can... (whatever they do)', so then you just call on them very easily, because you've got that very good relationship with them already."

Still an Honorary Fellow at UOW with very strong ties with academia, Winberg said she simply realised she wasn't going to achieve the outcomes she wanted to by following a purely academic career path, and when funding was secured to support her passion for the creation of a viable seaweed aquaculture venture in Australia, she knew she had to make the transition.

"It's an ideal situation now because I can operate, if you like, as an academic when I need to but also have the freedom and independence to put ideas into action through the Venus Shell Systems project."

Once again, Winberg credits conferences for helping her attract that funding, as well as funding for other projects she's been involved in along the way. She says there are strategic ways to approach conferences to make sure you are getting the outcomes you need.

"Personally I find it very difficult within the scientific field of research to garner interest in private funding, so I also attend other types of conferences, like the annual Biomarine Business Convention, which I've gone to for the past three years.

"They specifically bring in business interests and researchers from industry – rather than researchers from academia – because it's a conference event that really tries to focus on innovation and progress and private funding partnerships and outcomes."

She says that at Biomarine, outcomes are measured in terms of the number of deals or the dollar value of deals that were established at the conference and they set up very specific partnering schedules and programs during the conference.

"So I wanted to go and listen to some roundtable discussions on a particular area of interest, rather than just listen to research presentations from the keynote speakers, because they seem to have experts at these round table discussions.

"Parallel to that, they have one-to-one business meetings which you book online before you get to the conference. And then you have a schedule and a timetable of sitting down, like speed dating, I guess, and you target whether you want to talk to a company that might be interested in testing your product for a new medical application. Or you can sit down and

talk to investors or venture capitalists, so these types of conferences are also incredibly important too."

Winberg believes that, by regularly presenting your ideas at conferences, a range of investors come to understand the potential in what you are doing and you gain credibility.

"There can be a lot of hype in new industries, and it's very hard to tell the difference between people who know what they're talking about and those that don't and I think because you're recognized in the literature but also in attendance and speaking at conferences that investors – they actually feel more confident that, ah, this person is for real."

This became evident 12 months after the 2008 conference in Ireland, when she learned that conference organiser Stefan Kraan had been funded to put his own concepts into production.

"He got private funding after that conference and started a commercial company formulating seaweed ingredients for animal health.

"He now runs a very successful international company, Ocean Harvest, that improves feed for farmed salmon, thereby increasing the nutritional value passed on to humans. I never made a conscious decision to go down that same path, but I can certainly see similarities emerging now."

Professional friendships have been another important outcome from attending conferences. People she has met at conferences will visit her when they travel to Australia or she will arrange to catch up with them at a future conference. This is often on the basis that, even if there's not an immediate opportunity for some close collaboration, they will keep a professional friendship going because they feel that in a year or two there is going to be a real time and a place for working together. "You can just call on them very easily, because you've got that very good relationship with them."

With 800 million people worldwide suffering from chronic malnourishment, 3 million children under five dying each year from poor nutrition, and an anticipated global population of 9.6 billion by 2050, many feel one of our greatest challenges of the future will be finding ways to feed ourselves without compromising the environment and its resources.

And while it's still too early to tell what long-term outcomes or legacies there will be for the Shoalhaven region, Australia and the rest of the world, there are signs that Winberg's passion and determination, along with her strategic use of conferences to blend the world of science, industry, commerce, society and academia in order to achieve her vision, will be a significant, sustainable contribution as that future draws near.

THE **STORIES**

03

Bill Bowtell

Overcoming HIV/AIDS

Of the many contributions conferences can make to society, Professor Bill Bowtell believes none is more vital than the role they can play in promoting knowledge diffusion and information flow. Reflecting on the impact conferences had in the global effort to understand and address AIDS and HIV over the past 30 years, he states:

"I've seen people go to many types of conferences – you know, there are no doubt conferences for people who make sunglasses and they all come together and you improve sunglasses – but I know, in relation to AIDS, the conferences became the driving force behind massive changes in international and national policy that led to many people receiving treatment who otherwise would have died."

When Bob Hawke led the Labor Party to power in March 1983, and Bill Bowtell was appointed Chief of Staff (Senior Private Secretary) for then Minister for Health, Dr Neal Blewett, AIDS was emerging as a major health crisis internationally, and global concern was growing. The previous October, Australia's first case, an American tourist, had been diagnosed at Sydney's St Vincent's Hospital and a month after Labor took office the country was rocked by the news that the first Australian citizen had contracted AIDS. There was widespread community panic, as people searched for answers. Where had it come from? Who was at risk? How was it spread, and why was there no cure?

Looking back on this dynamic period, Bowtell says there were two very clear and very important objectives that dominated the health agenda: one was the implementation of the Medicare National Health Insurance Scheme (Medicare) by the Hawke government; and the other was management of the threat to public health with the emergence of the HIV and AIDS virus throughout the world.

"There was no cure of course; there was no treatment at all in the early days and there were a lot of very crazy and foolish responses that were being advocated by people in relation to how to deal with it, and people were getting sick and dying."

There were many small groups and working parties that had been operating for some years in various parts of the world that were inflicted with the disease, but with no central coordination their knowledge and experiences were isolated and at times ill-informed, and as community anger, fear and confusion grew alongside the growing number of identified cases, it was decided that an international approach was needed.

"More than in any other field I've ever been involved with there was an imperative need for people to come together in a conference internationally to compare notes, experiences, and understandings, to try to take [into consideration] the most recent scientific and medical research and explanations about what was going on."

But, far more importantly, according to Bowtell, was the way conferences became a focal point, bringing together all of the different groups, many of whom had very different perspectives about AIDS and how it should be managed.

"As it turned out, the scientists and the doctors had to collide with the people who were most affected by the virus: the gay men, injecting drug users, sex workers, people with haemophilia and other people who were first affected by this virus, and the mechanism for this coming together was the conferences."

The 1st International AIDS Conference was hosted by the US Department of Health and Human Services (HHS) and the World Health Organization (WHO) and held in Atlanta, Georgia, in April 1985. Two thousand people came together to contribute and learn, and so productive was the event that it was held annually until 1994 and biennially ever since. Even in the early years, the conferences would regularly attract anything up to 14 000 people (Berlin, 1993), and, as transportation and funding improved, conferences this century have attracted up to 26 000 (Toronto, 2006).

According to Bowtell, the first conferences became the venue for a titanic collision between everyone who was involved in the epidemic and the response.

"The first few [conferences] saw spectacular fireworks because the doctors and the scientists had one way of working and it was just inadequate to the task, and, as a profession, they certainly had no great ability to think

through what was needed to have the people most at risk of the virus change their behaviours and moderate it to prevent transmission. The orthodox medical profession is very good at treating illness, but very lacking in understanding [of how to prevent] illness in the first place.

"*So [the conferences were], if you like, the great collisions between the treatment and the research side, the orthodox side – doctors and scientists and so on – and the people who said it's got to be prevented, which was a social and political thing, and this led to some spectacular confrontations.*"

What became obvious as a result of these confrontations was that the problem needed not only medical and technical expertise to find the sources, modes of transmission, and the treatments and cures, but also policy responses that would bring about behavioural changes in the at-risk public.

"*You can argue that, of course, to deal with AIDS and other great problems you need scientists and researchers and clinicians and doctors who are technically able, and know what they're talking about, but you also need people who can shape the overall public policy response. I was a diplomat, with no medical or scientific background, but sheer luck placed me at the heart of the policy response required by the Australian government and it was far beyond the knowledge and capacity of doctors and scientists to bring about the changes in behaviour and awareness that were needed to contain the virus and the threat that it posed to our country.*"

It was as a result of these conferences that Bowtell says the different sides came closer to understanding the full spectrum of perspectives.

"*The conferences were the venue at which the international community, governments, scientists, doctors, clinicians, the World Health Organisation, media, private sector foundations and local communities came together to sort out what needed to be done and why and how.*"

"*Without the conferences there wouldn't have been anything like an effective international response. In addition to the international events, the Federal Government very swiftly instituted a series of National AIDS Conferences in Australia, from 1985 on, and from memory they would attract around*

5 000 delegates. There were also state and regional ones and these were the vehicles by which the information was transmitted and everyone came together to hammer out, debate, attack each other, really bring together all the politics and the information that was needed to respond to AIDS in Australia."

Without the luxury of the internet, people in many parts of the world were limited in the speed with which they could access the most current information, so the conferences became the medium through which the most recent advances or knowledge about the disease were publicised. Pharmaceutical companies would attend and talk about their most recent therapies or treatments and the media covered the conferences very closely, knowing everyone was hungry for the information each new conference would provide.

"We didn't have iPhones or the internet or podcasts or any of that sort of thing, and information was transmitted by documents and those documents were only available at the conferences and the papers were physical papers. People would also put up acetate slides or projections on the wall, so your physical presence at the conference was really important and people had to bring back reams of papers and these were distributed physically or by fax or whatever. So it was a very different working environment."

Bowtell believes the conferences were also a great opportunity for networking and establishing links with people at the forefront of the fight.

"Of course it was very important to go and meet the great international people like Jonathan Mann who is WHO and Tony Fauci and all of the famous scientists and doctors and activists, Larry Kramer and Dennis Altman, I mean everybody was in it. Even though it was terribly horrible and tragic, it was a lot of fun too, I've got to say. It was very exciting."

Apart from the 1986 Paris conference, following which Dr Bila Kapita, the Chief of Internal Medicine in Kinshasa, Zaire, was jailed for being the first public figure to talk openly about the problems his region was facing with AIDS, and the Durban conference in 2000 where Nelson Mandela during his closing address spoke of the irresponsibility of the South

African government in failing to face up to the AIDS crisis, one of the most significant things Bowtell believes the conference environment achieved was the provision of a platform for culturally sensitive issues to be openly debated, and for the realities of the situation to be made publicly known.

"These conferences became like the parliament of AIDS, but there was no rule book, so they had to be innovative and one of the main things they had to be innovative with was how to get people to talk about such sensitive issues as sex, drug use and prostitution.

"In the developed countries the way in which AIDS was transmitted was by sex and particularly by sex between men, gay sex, anal sex and by injecting drug use. So these conferences had to frankly and honestly talk about these things and it was not easy to do internationally and nationally. People did not necessarily want to hear about sex. And they certainly didn't want to talk about injecting drug use. There were very many taboos and in polite company these things would not be mentioned, much less be talked about on television.

"People had to say well, how do you talk about sex to 15 year old gay boys or clients of sex workers or sex workers themselves? How do you talk about the need for injecting drug users who mostly are doing something that's illegal to change practices by having needle and syringe exchanges, and access to clean needles and syringes? And how do you do this for the general population in countries where – including Australia – such things had never been openly discussed?

"So once it became clear that was what had to be done, and through the mechanisms of the conferences, people would come together and somebody from Peru might present and say, well, we're a very conservative country, predominantly Catholic and we found that this worked in our country. And somebody from the Netherlands would come and say, well, in relation to injecting drug use we were able to get these clean needle and syringe programmes up by stating this and that. And they would bring forward the evidence and say that when we did this the rate of new infections fell by such and such a level."

He also believes that by everyone coming together, having faced the same sorts of problems, they could look at the range of solutions and responses and see which ones worked and which ones didn't, and then facilitate rapid transmission of those that had worked.

Bowtell says the conferences enabled Australia to showcase our responses to the issue, many of which were replicated in other regions. Similarly, he said that our policy makers could see what others had done in their countries, which helped us tailor our approach to those of other cultures living within our borders.

"The conferences also helped us with policies, particularly in relation to non-English-speaking communities in Australia, because not only did we have to deal with the general Australian population and talking about these things, with so many different ethnic and language groups in Australia, we obviously had to take lessons about how we talk about these things say, in the Vietnamese community or in the Khmer community or in the Lebanese community because that would be different from how we deal with it in the general population."

Whilst he concedes that technological advances have meant access to information, and electronic networking opportunities are far greater than they were in the 80s, he says the potential benefits of conferences are just as great.

"The core of what conferences can achieve is still as relevant for me today, because I'm a great believer in going and meeting people and having a cup of coffee or dinner, and talking.

"It's all very well and good to have Skype calls and emails and teleconferences and that's great but it's no substitute for meeting people and talking to them face to face. It's better for all sorts of information, and of course, the more knowledge you have and the more people you meet who know more than you do or who are better than you are or who have more experience or better experience, of course, the more you know and the better you will do your job. How can that not be so? You can't lock yourself away in a room by yourself and expect to come up with policies that work.

"You might think you have a great idea but you have to take it to people who have experience and knowledge and they might say, 'yes, do this, do this but don't do that, we tried that and it failed'. So, yes, of course, they're just vital for professional development and for getting to a better solution faster, a better outcome more quickly."

And, according to Bill Bowtell, by bringing people together to share what they knew, by enabling the public to engage with the scientific community, and by helping those on all sides to understand the enormity of the issues, the International AIDS Conferences did just that.

"Where there were the changes that had to be made in sex and drug use and acknowledging what was happening there was, of course, a very strong reaction amongst religious fanatics and politicians and others who didn't like these things being talked about and who didn't want to face up to reality, and who would rather have had millions die thanks to entrenched bigotry and stupidity than come to terms with reality. But the media broadly did its job in ventilating all sides – and they were only able to do this in and around the vehicles of these conferences, where the huge arguments and the debates took place."

Bill Bowtell gives conferences a 10 out of 10. He believes they were one of the most important elements of the global response to AIDS, the success of which has significantly reduced the cost of the disease in terms of not only the dollars spent but of the lives saved, and that as the world grapples with new threats from things like the Ebola and Zika viruses, it will be to conferences that the world will turn to find the solutions we need.

THE **STORIES**

04

Ian Frazer

Development Of The
HPV Cervical Cancer Vaccine

It was 1982 and clinical immunologist Ian Frazer was presenting at a conference on genital warts when a colleague, Dr Gabrielle Medley, came up to him and said "you know, you should be looking for cancers caused by these viruses as well". Gabrielle made this suggestion because around this time Professor Harald zur Hausen in Germany had for the first time hypothesised that the human papillomavirus (HPV) might be responsible for cervical cancer.

"So that was where I got interested in the human papillomavirus and Gabrielle and I together defined that the rectal dysplasia in immune suppressed men was in fact papillomavirus related ... and it was the first major impact I had on the field."

That same year, another significant research collaboration was initiated at a gastroenterology conference, where Ian Frazer delivered a conference paper on his work on autoimmune liver disease. Later that day, he met Hans Meyer zum Buschenfelde who was also researching liver disease; the two struck up a friendship.

Having established a common interest in their research, he visited Professor zum Buschenfelde in 1984 at the German Council Research Institute (DKFZ). It was during this visit that he was introduced to Harald zur Hausen who was at the time head of the DKFZ. It was Hausen's early theories about the links between HPV and cancer that Gabrielle Medley had suggested he look into, so Frazer was thrilled to now speak face-to-face with the man he still refers to as "the father of research in HPV-associated cancer".

Over afternoon tea Ian Frazer and Harald zur Hausen shared their research interests, Hausen listening intently to what Frazer had to say about his rectal dysplasia studies, and Frazer becoming excited with the work Hausen was doing in relation to cervical cancer. It was then that Frazer became excited about the links between the body's defences against human papillomavirus and cervical cancer.

The inspiration, knowledge and motivation that came from that meeting gave both men a deeper understanding of the complexities and potential impacts of the virus, and propelled their respective areas of research forward. They collaborated regularly from then on – almost certainly bringing Frazer years closer to development of the HPV cervical cancer vaccine for which he is now famous.

When Frazer moved to Royal Brisbane Hospital as a clinical immunologist and University of Queensland Senior Lecturer in 1985, he continued to focus on this area, looking for ways our immune system could be managed or strengthened to resist this life-threatening virus.

So, for Professor Frazer, serendipitous meetings at conferences led to "real connections" that contributed to his development of the HPV vaccine some 20 years later. It is legacies such as this which have prompted Professor Frazer, 2006 Australian of the Year and a Companion in the Order of Australia, to stress the vital role that conferences play, particularly for younger researchers who need direct access to the latest developments in their fields and who need to establish important contacts and networks.

In fact, Professor Frazer would rate the importance of conferences in helping doctoral students and post-doctoral researchers get up to speed quickly and meet the right people as "...a 10 out of 10 and a mandatory part of the process". In terms of his own development, Frazer is convinced conferences have been integral to his career.

"I think they've been critically important (for me) – I mean, I would give them a 9 or 10 out of 10 for the process of getting me to where I am now."

It seems reasonable to assume that the link between Frazer, zum Buschenfelde, zur Hausen and the vaccine emerged as a direct result of the 1982 gastroenterology conference. Had that conference not taken place, the discovery of the vaccine, which has saved millions of women from HPV-related cancer since becoming widely available, would have been significantly delayed. It is also reasonable then to include those lives and the billions of dollars in medical treatment saved as measurable outcomes of that conference.

In 1981, Frazer, a Scottish-born renal physician, moved to Australia to work at the Walter and Eliza Hall Institute of Medical Research in Melbourne. From the beginning, he attended conferences on a regular basis to make contacts with people who had ideas he could incorporate into his own research and who had access to technologies that might be useful to the work he was doing.

"I was always looking for new ways of doing things and by actually talking to people who were doing the new ways of doing things that you didn't have access to then you learnt how to do them and if you didn't, then you learnt who could do them for you."

In the early 80s, for example, Frazer had read about ground-breaking work that was being done overseas in gene cloning, but no-one in Australia was using such technologies to work on papillomavirus. It wasn't until he attended a papillomavirus conference in 1986 in the United States where someone presented that they had cloned a relevant human gene in an expression vector (a cell) that he realised the significant impact such technology could have upon his own work.

And whilst these new ideas, new technologies and new approaches gleaned from conference experiences have profoundly influenced the direction his career has taken, by Frazer's own admission, it was the contacts, relationships and networks he made at those conferences that have proven the greatest legacy.

At the 1986 HPV conference in Georgetown, USA, for example, Frazer met fellow immunologist Margaret Stanley. At the time, they were the only two people in the room who seemed interested in the immunology of the virus, so whilst their interest in much of the conference content was somewhat limited, the information and knowledge they shared with each other over drinks was hugely beneficial.

"We spent a lot of time talking at the bar, as I recall, but that meeting has led to a long-standing friendship and reciprocal sabbaticals in each other's labs ... so the connections that came through the conferences were very real ... and many of the collaborations I have in the field of immunology have arisen from people I've met at conferences."

In 1989, Frazer went on sabbatical to Cambridge to try to learn more about the gene cloning technology he'd seen at the US conference three years earlier. Whilst there, he met Dr Jian Zhou, a Chinese virologist who had similar interests in cancer research. They began working together almost immediately, and by 1991 had found a way to manufacture the harmless outside shell of the HPV, which meant they had the basis for a vaccine to prevent cervical cancer. Although Zhou sadly passed away in 1999, he has posthumously shared in many of the prestigious awards bestowed upon Frazer since discovery of the vaccine.

As Professor Frazer insists, science is a collaborative effort, and whilst individuals may be recognised, it is essentially a team effort. Gabrielle Medley first urged him to look into the HPV cancer link, zur Hausen shared his knowledge, Margaret Stanley and other friends like Paul Lambert collaborated with him over the years, and Frazer's own team of scientists, researchers and students back in his lab at the University of Queensland worked tirelessly as they inched towards the vaccine's development. Each of these key individuals have played a part in steering Ian and his team towards their discoveries – and conferences, too, have played a significant role in bringing them and their ideas into Frazer's life.

Despite reaching lofty heights – including being named a National Living Treasure by the National Trust of Australia (2012) and winning the European Inventor Award (2015) – Frazer is not standing still. For, while the HPV vaccine available today can protect those who have never been exposed to the virus, Frazer and his team are now working on ways to prevent those who've already contracted the virus from going on to develop cancers. His other important area of research is looking into squamous cell skin cancers and how papillomavirus evades the immune system in the skin. And, again, Frazer is making use of conference platforms to drive his research forward.

"I certainly think that quite a large part of the collaborations we're doing at the moment have come out of meeting people at conferences. The bigger team that we're involved with now basically involves every discipline that you can think of in biomedical research from Ecogenomics through to Bioinformatics, and yes, I meet up with these people through conferences."

Frazer is also making use of conferences to help him find funding. Sadly, according to Frazer, governments in Australia see research in three-year blocks, but finding cures for things like cancer takes long-term, significant funding commitments that usually only major pharmaceutical companies are willing to make. So, Frazer and his team make regular trips to overseas conferences to showcase their findings and look for organisations that are willing to back them for the long haul.

"The conferences are where we go to try and partner with [these] companies who are interested in vaccine development. We also get a chance to see what the opposition is doing."

Some conferences are designed for partnering such as Bio and Ausbio where, "basically," he jests, "it's a meat market, if you like, where everybody presents their stuff to the companies. The point is if you've got something of interest the chances are that the people that you really want to speak to will be at the conference and you can have a quiet chat in the corner and say can we come along and pitch to your company?" Then Frazer and his team do road shows from the contacts that they've made at these conferences.

While Frazer acknowledges the considerable costs involved in organising and running a conference, he says that the costs of sending staff can prove an enormous burden for organisations. He believes the challenge for conference organisers is to keep the relevance there without making the costs so high that few can afford to attend.

"The first conference I went to, you found your own accommodation, there was no registration fee, you just turned up and you bought your own food and that was fine, not a problem. When I ran the International Papillomavirus workshop down in Southport in 1996 we had a registration fee which included meals and accommodation which was about $400. Now you're looking upwards of $2,500 to $3,000 for that sort of package and that makes it very difficult to send lots of students there, so I think the critical thing for getting good engagement is to be flexible about the sort of packages that are available [so more people can attend]."

The other piece of advice he gave was that conference organisers need to be clear about their purpose. He said that small, boutique conferences which are highly focused and topic-specific will attract all the major players, but to be successful they need to be led by an expert in the field.

"Then there are the big conferences that everybody comes to, like AACR or the Australasian Society for Immunology conferences where the aim is to provide a broad education for people starting out, and the critical thing there is to have keynote speakers who will attract people to come along."

Finally, this humble but knowledgeable man wanted to stress how important he believes it is for Australia to host big international conferences, not because it puts Australia on the map or for any short-term economic benefit from tourism, but because of the exposure, education and opportunities it gives our next generation of high achievers.

"It's really nice to have all the talent here, and I think [it] should be remembered that if you want Australia still to be leading in a field then it's really important that the international conferences come here, because then you bring all the people who are going through the process of becoming qualified as researchers together, and it exposes them to the people who really matter at the time and that's critical in their development. That can't be underestimated for value."

THE **STORIES**

05

Martin Green

'The Father Of Photovoltaics'

This century we've already experienced 15 of the 16 hottest years on record, with 2011–2015 being the warmest five-year period in recorded history. In March 2016, the US-based National Oceanic and Atmospheric Administration announced global temperatures had smashed records for the 10th straight month, and while the run of broken records is worrying enough, it is the margin by which those records were broken that is of most concern. February, for example, jumped 2.18 degrees above the previous average, which is an unprecedented spike considering records are usually only broken by hundredths or tenths of a degree, and leading meteorologists attribute at least half of this spike to global warming.

While climate scientists, politicians and industry struggle to reach consensus on the best way to respond to global warming, some fear this accelerated rate of heating could be an indicator we've done too little, too late. What almost everyone does agree upon, however, is that global warming is a reality, that the primary driver of this unprecedented level of climate change is human activity, and that urgent societal response is essential. In other words, reducing emissions and finding new ways to meet our power needs is crucial in order to save ourselves from a likely global environmental catastrophe.

Every hour the sun beams more than enough energy to Earth to satisfy global needs for an entire year, yet it currently generates only about 1 per cent of our electricity. So, when the man who has led the world in the race to capture and covert that energy into electricity for the past 30 years tells you that conferences were a constant and critical motivator that pushed him towards his achievements, it's important to ask why.

Professor Martin Green (OAM) has received countless awards for his lifetime of work developing and improving the efficiency of solar cells, including the 2002 Right Livelihood Award (Alternative Nobel Prize), the 2004 World Technology Award for Energy, and the 2016 Australian Academy of Science's prestigious Ian Wark Medal and Lecture. He spearheads an extensive research team at the University of NSW (UNSW) that is set to revolutionise the global energy industry, and happily admits conferences have played a very important part in that team's ongoing success.

"I think [conferences] have been critical because they've pushed our research along.

"Conferences were the opportunity to show off your new results ... so they were always a big motivator for everyone to try to get the best results in before a conference. Having a conference was like having a focal point for what you were doing in your research. Often there'd be a jump in your achievements the month or two before a conference because everyone strove to get the best results [to be able to] report on them at the conference."

A graduate of the University of Queensland, Green started his career in micro-electronics, but began losing interest in what he then saw as being mainly development of consumer entertainment products (TV/radio components etc.). Driven by an urge to do something more meaningful and challenging, he started looking into the (then) fledgling area of photovoltaics (cells which can convert sunlight directly into energy). When the 1973 oil embargo raised questions and concerns in the US about our social and economic dependence on this expensive and limited resource, interest and support for alternative energy research such as Green's increased. He and his colleagues at UNSW fabricated their first solar cell there in 1975 and the following year organised a trip to the IEEE Photovoltaic Specialists Conference being held in the US to present on their results.

They saw the trip as an opportunity to learn everything they could about the latest developments in their field, and prepared a hectic itinerary for the weeks prior to and following the conference. They tried to visit two research groups or start-up companies related to photovoltaics per day, and took on board any advice that was offered.

"It was quite unusual to have three Aussies drop in on you in the US back then. We made a huge number of contacts, and those we met didn't mind going out of their way if you wanted some special silicon wafers to make a cell or something. We learned about the latest things that were happening, but also how their labs were set up and how we should be setting up our own; the infrastructure we needed etc."

Essentially, they used the conference experience to piggyback their broader quest for knowledge and to satisfy three primary objectives: to take in the widest range of information from other sources as possible; to create interest in (and possibly support for) their own work; and to establish working and research partnerships.

"Those opportunities definitely wouldn't have been there if it hadn't been for the conference. People we met on that trip really helped us along. They remembered us afterwards too, and it's been a big part of our history. I'm still in contact with many of these people and even today still work with some of them."

Green and his team returned from the conference inspired. In 1977 they used what they'd learned to develop their own lab and began striving to break what was then known as 'the four minute mile' of photovoltaics: a solar cell efficiency level of 20 per cent. In what seemed to Green to be a race between UNSW and the rest of the world, they quickly leapt ahead, leaving even NASA and COMSAT in their wake. Over the next few years they stayed on top, constantly inching their way towards the 20 per cent target with modifications like reducing the area of contact points between the silicon and the metal, or reducing reflection rates by adding texture to the surface of the cell. In 1985, Green and his team were the first to reach that magical benchmark, and ever since have continued to push the boundaries of the technology, most notably by developing ways to transfer cell efficiency into low-cost production of solar panels. They've broken record after record, as they developed more effective ways of situating and configuring the cells, and in 2014 managed to achieve a remarkable efficiency level of 40 per cent.

By Green's own admission, conferences have played an essential part in this success. As well as the immediate motivational benefits, conferences have been integral to his achievements in terms of providing inspiration and ideas, networks and staffing, and in securing funding for research.

"It's inspiring to meet with like-minded people who are working in the same areas, and it helps to keep everyone interested. There's a real community there that's mainly self-directed, so picking up information quickly I guess is one of the key benefits of conferences."

Green also believes conferences were helpful in attracting the best new talent for his research teams, admitting he was often approached by post-doctoral students or new graduates interested in his work.

"Conferences were a way for academic supervisors to introduce you to their favourite students and ask whether that student could come out here to do some work. I've personally supervised over 70 research students, and that was quite a natural way of being introduced to someone."

Green has always ensured his staff and students had opportunities to attend conferences to broaden their knowledge base.

"It used to be hard to get funding to attend conferences, so students largely had to pay their own way, but now they can apply for funding through the university so they're attending more often. It's really good for them to be able to make contacts both for their own research they're doing here and for their future career and that's a really important part of their education; conference attendance."

Many of Green's past students have gone on to lead solar technology companies across the globe, particularly in China and throughout Asia. Demand for solar cells began increasing quickly in the early 2000s, creating the potential for quick expansion, so there was plenty of US financial backing for those start-ups that looked like they knew what they were doing. According to Green, one of the main criteria used to assess a company's viability was "whether they had contact with good technology such as at UNSW, so a lot of those companies appointed Chief Technology Officers that had trained here with us."

"They were mainly students from a Chinese background, but not all, and that means there's literally dozens of companies with past students running them who learnt most [of what] they know about solar here and who see us as a likely source of new knowledge on where they should be heading."

Another important benefit of conferences for Green was the opportunities they gave him to make contacts and establish networks. Along with other leading scientists like Nobel Laureate Professor Brian Schmidt (astronomer), Green admits his approach to success is to focus on competing internationally. He says that international links are important to Australia's success and that conferences definitely were the vehicle through which most of those links were forged.

"The networking aspects of conferences are quite important; often more so than what you learned technically.

"You might get to talk to people outside your own area and get an update on areas you're not as familiar with. I find that very useful. Some people I got to know through conferences but at the time I wasn't too interested in what they were doing, but since then our work has become so broad that they're now in our collaborative team."

Another strategy Green employed to ensure he got the most from a conference was to try to present his research as early in the program as possible.

"That's important because then if people are interested in one aspect of your work or another they come up to you throughout the conference and you have more chances of meeting them at the social functions and other networking events."

And whilst conferences were the catalyst for most of his international connections, they also helped him to develop close ties with local people he would otherwise not have sat and talked with.

"Even local people – some working in Melbourne – you don't get a chance to see them very often, but if you're travelling to a conference together and you realise you're both Australian you're more likely to meet up and talk with each other."

An ongoing concern for Green and his team throughout the years, however, was funding. Despite their remarkable record of success, the huge costs involved in maintaining a large research project such as theirs meant they needed to constantly source research grants and financial partnerships. In the early 1980s they realised they needed more funding than could be sourced locally, so they made it an objective to get overseas funding through conferences.

"The people in charge of giving out funding would cotton onto the idea that we were doing useful work when they saw the presentations we gave at conferences.

"They'd then meet with us to see what could be done in terms of them organising funding and that kind of thing. We received one grant from NASA in the early 1980's that tied us over for a while but between when Reagan was elected and the Chernobyl accident occurred funding got quite tight and we were struggling to maintain the activity levels we'd built up. We got several grants from the US Department of Energy in the late 80's, organised through conferences we went to and the international contacts we'd made at previous conferences, so they were very important."

He also noted that funding support from industry can come about as a result of conferences.

"Some conferences now have very large exhibitions associated with them, particularly in Europe, so there's a good chance to catch up with industry people. There's been a lot of funding from industry organised through conferences over recent years."

Green, whose research centre (the Australian Centre for Advanced Photovoltaics) is now funded by the Australian National Energy Agency (ARENA), says another important aspect with regard to funding was the way links and contacts made through conferences could be used to demonstrate international collaboration, particularly important in terms of success of funding applications in Australia.

"Funding bodies here in Australia seem focussed on encouraging collaboration. There is pressure on you to collaborate and on most funding applications it is the collaboration aspect that attracts the support."

He said that when he applied for funding to establish the centre, he approached the strongest groups in the photovoltaic research area in the country and put in a combined application to demonstrate how they would be collaborating.

"We knew that was a better strategy than each group applying individually, trying to blow each other out of the water."

And whilst Green is clearly an avid believer in the long-term and significant benefits of conferences, he admits hosting them can be hard work. He and his team hosted the 1989 International Photovoltaic Conference in Sydney, which he says people still mention decades later.

"It was quite demanding on our research group but it created a very favourable impression of Australia in the minds of the people that attended and increased our international standing.

"More people became aware of what we were doing and people have been on at me ever since to organise another one but so far I've shied away. We're so well-known now we don't really need the publicity or exposure, but if we were a smaller group that publicity can be an important benefit from hosting a conference."

Green believes we have great capacity, resources and skills in Australia to host conferences, and people like to come here – but it is challenging to travel from Europe and areas of the US. He believes having good speakers who can convey a lot of information quickly without getting bogged down in detail, plenty of interaction and a well thought out program are three key ingredients of a good conference.

He also sees great benefit, particularly for Australia, in combining conferences with other activities or events, such as the conferences organised by UNSW to coincide with the Sydney Olympics, the European conferences which partner with industry exhibitions, or in wider consultative opportunities/programs such as those he organised for his own trip to the US back in the 70s.

With Australia and its near neighbours in the firing line in terms of the impacts of climate change, Professor Green and his team have made all the right moves to situate Sydney as the photovoltaic technology and educational hub for the Asia-Pacific region. Indeed, there is increasing evidence to suggest it is now technically and economically feasible that our energy systems could run entirely on renewables (water, wind and solar) –

were the social, political, financial and perceptual barriers to be overcome. And thanks to the knowledge gleaned and the international links forged mainly through conferences, Green and his colleagues have turned Australian 'smarts' into manufacturing realities with the potential to make a significant difference as we work to solve this crucial global problem.

THE **STORIES**

06

Tom Calma

Advancing Rights For Indigenous Australians

According to organisations such as Oxfam, the Australian Human Rights Commission and the World Health Organization, indigenous people in many parts of the world remain significantly disadvantaged when compared to their non-indigenous counterparts. Australia has been identified as one of the slowest of the developed nations to implement policies and strategies for improving living standards for its indigenous peoples.

Ever since colonisation, Indigenous Australians have been marginalised and, until the 1960s, had been excluded from many of the social rights afforded other citizens, including access to welfare, pensions and industrial award conditions and wages, the right to be regarded as equal to other citizens in the eyes of the law, the right to be acknowledged and included in the national census, and even the right to vote.

In the struggle for change, Indigenous Australians have long led the way, using activism, workshops and conferences to raise awareness and protest against inequality, injustice, dispossession of land and protectionist policies. One of the earliest examples of this is the Day of Mourning declared by the Aboriginal Progressive Association on 26 January 1938. It marked the first of many such gatherings, over many decades.

In the field of education, successive state and commonwealth governments have imposed various education strategies upon Indigenous Australians, such as the NSW Aborigines Act of 1909, which prohibited Aboriginal children from attending public schools. Without any consultation or collaboration, Aboriginal children only 'schools' were then established on reserves and, more often than not, the reserve manager's untrained wife would teach from syllabuses that focused on manual or domestic servitude training.

In 1940 responsibility for the education of Aboriginal people was transferred to the Department for Education, which took control of reserve buildings and started to provide trained teachers. By 1950 Aboriginal children began assimilating into mainstream public schools, but it wasn't until the establishment of the NSW Aboriginal Education Consultative Group (AECG) in 1976 and the National Aboriginal Education Committee in 1977, along with the numerous conferences they conducted over the following decades, that positive changes in the approach to education for Indigenous children were implemented.

The Aboriginal Education Conferences of the 1980s and 1990s enabled Aboriginal leaders and experts to have a say in the education of both Indigenous and non-Indigenous children, and paved the way for the improved outcomes we see today, such as a doubling of the number of Indigenous students enrolled in tertiary education, and Year 12 retention rates for Indigenous students up from 32 per cent in the late 1990s to 60 per cent in 2014.

Professor Tom Calma AO, now Chancellor of the University of Canberra, was involved with those early conferences, and says they gave people from a diverse range of backgrounds the opportunity to talk about the issues that mattered, and became one of the key drivers behind the social and political shifts that have occurred for Indigenous Australians over the past 40 years.

"There's quite a number of senior Indigenous academics now and leaders in academia who went through and attended those conferences, and they were really important in terms of Aboriginal policy formulation and debate."

An Aboriginal elder from the Kungarakan tribal group and a member of the Iwaidja tribal group whose traditional lands are south-west of Darwin and on the Coburg Peninsula in the Northern Territory, Tom has been involved in Indigenous affairs at all levels for over 45 years, including serving as Aboriginal and Torres Strait Islander Social Justice Commissioner from 12 July 2004 to 31 January 2010.

He believes the Aboriginal Education Conferences marked the start of real change for Indigenous Australians and that the impacts are being seen today in the improved educational outcomes being realised.

"They started off at probably a few hundred people but grew to four or five hundred at some of the conferences, and we had speakers like Eddie Mabo, who was involved in education at the time, and some prime movers and big power-brokers like Linda Burney, who was Chair of the NSW Aboriginal Education Consultative Group.

"The Commonwealth Department of Education had Aboriginal education as its number one major policy reform back then, so there was federal funding for these conferences, but they were run by the Aboriginal people ourselves, which worked well."

As a result of these conferences, Indigenous Education Policies that focused on things like the importance of Indigenous studies for all Australians, the promotion of cross-cultural understanding, and ensuring that Aboriginal people were involved in the future direction and management of their own education were established, and those policies influenced the way Australia's history was taught in the classroom. Importantly, the conferences focused on all tiers of education and all geographic areas.

Professor Calma has an impressive list of appointments, awards and achievements to his credit including the roles of Co-Chair of Reconciliation Australia, Chair of the Close the Gap (CTG) steering committee for Indigenous Health Equality (2006–2010) and Senior Advisor to Immigration and Indigenous Affairs Minister, Philip Ruddock, on Indigenous affairs (2003). He received an Order of Australia in 2012 for distinguished service to the Indigenous community, and for his advocacy of human rights and social justice.

Throughout his years as a social advocate, Calma says he consistently used conferences as a platform to educate those in the audience about the gamut of associated issues he believed were important.

"If I'm given a topic to speak about at a conference, I do talk about it but I'll also bring in a whole range of other issues and try to present what we call a determinant or a social determinant perspective. So when we talk about Indigenous health, for example, and prisoners, or our people being incarcerated, you need to discuss the very high proportion who have mental health issues or who have experienced a lot of intergenerational trauma and issues impacting their life like fetal alcohol spectrum disorder or other general health issues, to overcrowded housing, to lack of education, lack of employment and so on. These are the things that bring them into contact with the justice system."

He says a lot of his presentations take a holistic approach and bring in human rights or social justice approaches to look for solutions.

"All of these other issues like unemployment, housing, crime, alcohol etc. have got to be considered when you look at health or you look at justice issues or you look at education, and it's not as simple as some people like to present."

In terms of the importance of the role of conferences in facilitating the dissemination of information and knowledge in his area, Calma says they sit at about 7 or 8 out of 10, depending on how they are run and the way presenters and audience members approach the opportunity.

"As a presenter I'd give conferences around about seven or eight out of ten but it really depends on the conference and what people are willing to put into it.

"I think there's always a difference between what one presenter gets out of a conference and what others do. I'm one who will never, if I can help it, do a presentation and then leave. I will always stay around for at least half a day at a conference and give people an opportunity to have a chat and follow up on any issues or I try to attend a session or two and it really frustrates me when people breeze in and breeze out. It's not good for achieving outcomes. I suppose it's all just personal approaches but that's the way I like to operate."

He says talking to people at conferences also helps him to gauge whether important messages are being understood by the general public.

"Every conference I present at – and I present at a lot – I always get very positive feedback, but I also get to find out how many people still don't know about important initiatives like the Close The Gap campaign, and how many people don't understand what social determinants are, so I'm always pushing that agenda and conferences have helped get a lot of people involved in those things."

Close the Gap is a strategy that aims to achieve health equality in terms of life expectancy, child mortality, education and employment outcomes. Developed in response to the 2005 Human Rights Commission Social Justice Report, it is a formal commitment endorsed by the Australian Government and monitored by the Council of Australian Governments

(COAG) to achieve health equality within 25 years.

Another important observation of Calma's, when reflecting upon his conference experiences, was a notable under-representation of women on expert panels and in keynote speaker roles.

"At one recent health conference I was at, I was on a panel of speakers comprised of only men.

"I pointed out to the organizers that they needed to be conscious of involving more women, and they took my comments well, but they have to be more conscious of these things.

"There's plenty of meritorious women around who can talk on these issues probably more eloquently and authoritatively than some of the men, and organisers should always be aware – get smarter on some of these things – because, is it a lack of consciousness or is it just discriminatory? With this case it wasn't discrimination, because there were a number of women on the committee that selected the panel; they just didn't even think about it."

He says, whilst some conferences are just about distributing information or advising people what is available to them, the most memorable ones for him were those that set out to bring about social change or achieve specific outcomes.

"If you look at something like the Public Health Association of Australia (PHAA) conferences, or the important Suicide Prevention Australia (SPA) conferences I'm involved with, at the end of them, we develop up a set of outcomes and recommendations and they include research and advocacy and they establish partnerships with funding bodies."

As one of the inaugural White Ribbon Ambassadors, one such memorable conference for Calma was the 2012 Indigenous Men's Conference at Ross River, just south of Alice Springs.

"It was more of a summit than a conference, I suppose, but it was very good and some very good outcomes came out of that, where men really declared their position on supporting other men standing up against violence against women.

"You just see all of these issues that are confronting us all the time and people become very blasé about it or defensive or it's just not in their consciousness and I think it's important to raise these things all the time."

Another important outcome that he attributes to his involvement with conferences was Canada's adoption of Australia's Close the Gap strategy which seeks to reduce the equity gap between indigenous and non-indigenous populations in a number of key areas.

As a result of his work trying to reduce tobacco use in Indigenous communities, he was asked to deliver the keynote address at the 2009 Oceania Tobacco Control 09 Conference in Darwin. The conference brought together people tackling tobacco-related issues from New Zealand, Australia and parts of Asia. Impressed by what he had to say, the Australian Department of Health invited Calma to work with them, and in 2010 he was invited to Canada to talk about tobacco control with people from the Assembly of First Nations. This assembly brings together Chiefs from all the First Nation bands in Canada and works to protect the Aboriginal and treaty rights and interests of their people, particularly in the areas of health, culture, education and language.

"They invited me there to talk about tobacco control, but while I was there I also talked about what we were doing in Australia with the CTG campaign. I explained how we'd approached it in terms of the relationships we developed between the governments and Indigenous peoples, and then early in 2011 the National Chiefs in Canada had discussions about what we'd done, and started their own CTG program in Canada. They also declared March 22 as International CTG Day, which is pretty much the same date as our own CTG Day."

Later in 2011, the Assembly invited Calma back to Canada to address the first Indigenous Health Conference they'd had in 10 years.

"It was a big gathering, and again I talked about our CTG program. The next year, in 2012, they met with the Canadian Prime Minister and declared that they wanted a similar arrangement to what we had in Australia. They also announced they would run CTG continually, which they've done ever since, so from just a conference address and then a couple

of conversations, conference presentations and workshops in Canada, the CTG campaign was able to get up and running over there."

Real change had been made.

"That was probably the most memorable or significant conference outcome; being able to work with them to develop the strategies, and having been able to influence the way they approached the government. For me, that was a very personally rewarding outcome."

Conferences also played a big part in Calma's role as a Senior Diplomat between 1995 and 2002 when he was charged with the task of formally developing Australia's educational interests overseas.

One of five Senior Diplomats sent to various regions of the world to determine what potential there was for Australia to capitalise upon the burgeoning international education market, Calma spent time in both India and Vietnam.

"Every year the five of us would come back and run conferences in every state and territory so that all the education providers, both higher education, VET and schools, could come together and get intelligence about what was happening offshore and how they should go about their business."

Calma says these conferences played a pivotal role in enabling Australia to establish itself in the international student market.

"That was really the beginning of the big international education movement and for fee-paying students to study in Australia, and I was lucky to be able to do that job.

"We saw how arrangements could be developed across the world, and we're seeing the outcomes of those relationships now. In 1995 when I first went overseas, the international student market was worth just under a billion dollars and now it's worth over $19 billion; it's a major international export."

Named *The Bulletin* magazine's Most Influential Indigenous Australian in 2007, *GQ* magazine's Man of Inspiration in 2008, and the ACT's Australian of the Year in 2013, Tom Calma has a reputation as a leading Indigenous scholar who has worked tirelessly to remove barriers and advance living standards for Australia's Indigenous peoples. By his own admission, much of what he has done in terms of advocacy and public education has been achieved by using conferences as a platform to raise awareness and gather momentum for change. He believes conferences have played an important role in the development of current programs and policies aimed at improving Indigenous peoples' quality of life and the issues that impact on their lives. He concluded:

"For me, conferences are fantastic because they really do raise awareness, especially those that are well supported by the corporate sector. They are also a great venue to advance reconciliation and develop greater social, cultural and political understandings of Australia's Indigenous populations generally."

THE **STORIES**

07

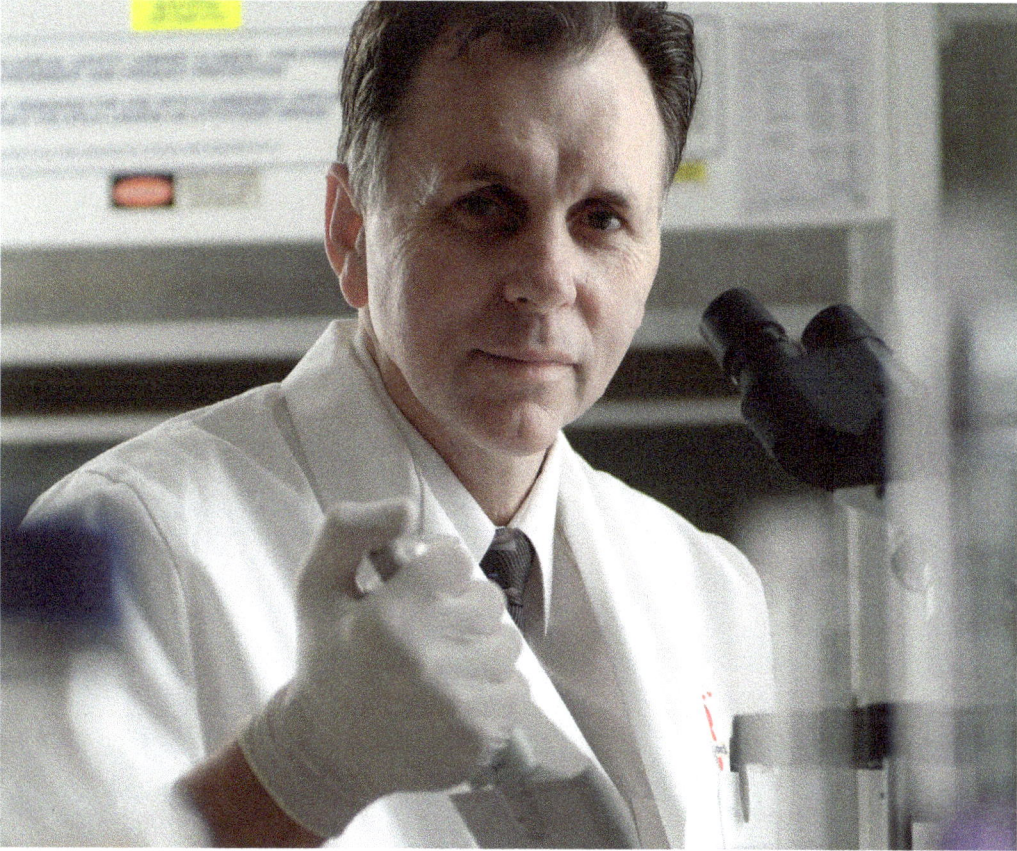

Barry Marshall

Treating Stomach Ulcers

Every day, in clinics and laboratories across the globe, thousands of doctors, researchers and scientists venture quietly on voyages of discovery as they seek to answer the mysteries of our time. Most build on previous knowledge, making small but useful contributions to their field and attracting little in terms of public recognition, but for a fortunate few, the secrets they unlock are of such global significance, they are honoured as thought-leaders of their generation.

One such individual of recent times is Barry Marshall, who in 1981 found evidence to support his theory that peptic ulcers and most stomach cancers were caused by bacteria.

But rather than being welcomed, the discovery was initially ridiculed and rejected by many in the medical community, who had long held that such conditions were the result of lifestyle factors such as excessive stress and a rich or spicy diet.

At only 31, with the future of his medical career, and a wife and four young children to consider, Marshall could easily have buckled under the weight of the 'expert' criticism being levelled against him. However, certain that hundreds of thousands of ulcer sufferers were being given unnecessary medications and surgeries each year, he chose instead to use conference presentations, meetings and associated research papers to fight to make his findings known.

Now a Nobel Laureate, Marshall enjoyed a relatively humble upbringing, born to teenaged working class parents in the gold mining town of Kalgoorlie, 800 kilometres east of Perth. Living above his Grandfather's pub/TAB, he quickly learned good money could be made scouring the floors and grounds of the pub for dropped cash, and if he was bored he'd tag along behind Bertie, the pub's heavy-drinking yardman, as he went about the business of beheading chooks and chopping wood.

When he was old enough to venture out into the neighbourhood, he and his mates tested out homemade catapults and bows and arrows, as they rode around on their bikes, or made fireworks in each other's backyards. His mother's nursing and medical books entertained him on rainy days, and when he was able to, he watched on as his highly skilled fitter-and-turner father showed him all there was to know about making engines, machines and other things 'work'.

Worried her sons would end up in the mines if they stayed in Kalgoorlie, Marshall's mother insisted the family move to Perth in 1958, and when he found himself in the seaside suburb of Scarborough, young Marshall discovered new ways to sustain his adventurous spirit, fossicking through the nearby second-hand metal yard, and snorkelling or surfing around the rocks at the local beach.

"Being the oldest I suppose I was pretty much left to myself a lot of the time as a child and I guess I liked to live dangerously," he told broadcaster Norman Swan in an interview in 2008.

"I learned that things could always be risky and things could always go wrong, but I learned to be a risk taker."

It seems he also learned where there was a will, there was a way, and he learned to never give up when faced with a challenge.

"I felt there was nothing out there that I couldn't do if I had a go at it and learned enough about it," he told Swan.

And it was most likely that adventurous, risk-taking, but determined, spirit that drove Marshall to stand with confidence against the bulk of the medical community and the power of the global pharmaceutical giants when he discovered the real cause of ulcers.

Remarkably, exactly a century before Marshall's discovery, pathologist Edwin Klebs had noticed the appearance of bacteria-like organisms inside the gastric glands of those with ulcers. Over the next 60 years, a number of studies and research papers identified links between this particular bacterium – *Helicobacter pylori* (HP) – and ulcers, but because of the strongly held belief within gastric medicine that bacteria couldn't survive the stomach's acid environment, such findings were largely ignored.

In 1940 another young doctor examining pieces of stomach removed during a range of different operations identified a significantly increased prevalence of this bacterium in ulcer patients and wondered whether there was a link. Like Marshall, Dr Al Freedberg had only been out of medical school a few years at the time, and although he went on to become a leading cardiologist, developing one of the earlier treatments for angina, his pioneering work and research publications on stomach ulcers was largely ignored.

In a *New York Times* interview a few years before his death in 2009, the 101-year-old admitted he'd always been "very upset" that colleagues, including his own boss at the time, thought he was wrong and discouraged him from continuing the research.

Marshall himself said in 2005 that he believed Freedberg "would have won the Nobel Prize in about 1951, just as I was getting born," had he been able to pursue his line of investigation into ulcers.

Fortunately, 40 years later, when Marshall and his research partner, pathologist Robin Warren, found fragments of evidence suggesting that, for some reason, *Helicobacter pylori* could live happily within the stomach, and perhaps could be the cause of ulcers, Marshall's inquisitive and tenacious spirit induced them to keep probing. With his knowledge of electronics and computing, Marshall built his own computer, giving himself access to the latest international research, information about grants and funding opportunities, as well as the ability to print and submit consent forms and protocols for his research.

The pair developed their hypothesis, and in 1982 set about proving it. One of the first steps was to try to produce a culture of the bacteria, which proved unexpectedly difficult until fate lent a hand. Their usual procedure was for the lab technician to check the petri dishes in the incubator every two or three days; if no culture had grown in that time, they would be discarded. On the Friday before Easter, a locum technician forgot this routine procedure, and the long weekend holiday meant the dishes weren't removed from the incubator until the following Tuesday. This five-day incubation period proved crucial: when next checked, the culture had grown.

This fortunate piece of luck meant the bacteria could now be isolated, named, studied and replicated for their research.

"We figured out how Helicobacter pylori could live in the stomach by hiding in the thick, acid-resistant layer of mucus that coats the stomach wall, and we could play around with it in the test tube, doing all kinds of useful experiments. We also quickly learned which antibiotics could kill it."

But these developments fell far short of impressing the wider medical community. In his Nobel Prize biography, Marshall wrote:

"In October 1982 I presented the preliminary findings from our study to the local College of Physicians meeting, where it received a mixed response. I found that my contract at Royal Perth would not be renewed the following year."

Fortunately, however, there were also some who were very interested in what Marshall had to say. Norm Marinovich and Ian Hislop, both doctors at Fremantle Hospital, the smallest of Perth's three teaching hospitals, approached Marshall with an offer of a Senior Registrar's position and urged him to join their research team to continue his work. Over the next few years they began using certain antibiotics to treat patients with peptic ulcers, achieving excellent results.

They continued to unravel the secrets of this mysterious bacterium and carefully documented their successes from their trials. But Marshall says even with this mounting body of evidence, speaking out and changing the opinions of the establishment or the status quo wasn't easy.

He and Warren had proven the existence of *H. pylori*, they could explain how it survived in the stomach, and they even had evidence that antibiotics could eradicate it and relieve the symptoms of sufferers, but still critics argued there was no proof it could actually cause an ulcer, and insisted it had most likely invaded the stomach only after the ulcer had weakened the patient's immune system.

This was one of the main lines of argument put forward by the drug companies. At that time, about 10 per cent of the global adult population were suffering from ulcers, and the ulcer-drug (acid blocker) business was worth three to five billion dollars each year. According to Marshall, these large corporations were understandably acting in the interests of their shareholders.

"As far as they were concerned, people had ulcers all their life," he told Swan, *"and so their projection was, 'If we start you on drugs for your ulcer you will need to spend $1 to $3 a day for the next 10 or 20 years to keep your ulcer under control'.*

"If suddenly ulcers could be cured and it became unnecessary to take these drugs all the time, the share value would go down by three-quarters, so they didn't want to support us, and they did all kinds of other research trying to prove that bacteria did not cause ulcers.

"Basically they said 'No ... You get ulcers, so your immune system is weakened, and then you get the bacteria'.

"They were very sceptical."

The established international gastroenterological community also found it difficult to accept that a young general physician and a pathologist from Perth could have proven their entire branch of medicine had been on the wrong track in the treatment and management of ulcers for so long. The lack of support from colleagues in Australia stung Marshall the most:

"The worst day in the whole lot of it was the rejection letter from the Australian gastroenterologists back in 1983," he later said in a 2008 interview.

When it had become clear to Marshall and Warren that they'd made an incredibly important discovery, the duo wrote a two-page letter to *The Lancet* (one of the world's oldest and best known general medical journals) to stake their claim to the discovery. Once that was in press, they took the same information and created an abstract for a presentation they wanted to make at the Australian Gastroenterological Society's meeting to be held in Perth later that year.

"Back in 1983 five hundred dollars was a lot to spend on an airfare to Melbourne or the east coast of Australia, but with the meeting being in Perth we could afford it, and we had a vision of presenting our amazing discovery about the cause of ulcers to the world."

But instead of being welcomed to speak at the conference, they were dismayed to be told their abstract had been rejected.

"We were sent the standard letter: 'Dear Dr Marshall … So many submissions … yours was ranked 67th and we could only accept 57 …' the letter read. I still have that letter, and I always tell researchers to keep your rejections in a bottom drawer and years later you may be able to show them to your students, as I do."

Disappointed, Marshall went to his supervisor at Fremantle Hospital, microbiologist David McGechie, who decided to contact Dr Martin Skirrow, a renowned microbiologist from England, who he knew was interested in bacteria similar to the ones Marshall had cultured. The pair quickly created strong professional links, and Skirrow worked quickly to bring Marshall to Brussels, to make his first presentation at the European Campylobacter meeting in September 1983.

That presentation was well received, and set the scene for a major article to be printed in *The Lancet*, seven months later.

As the weight of evidence grew, so too did Marshall's confidence that they were right, but detractors' claims that *H. pylori* was simply an 'opportunistic' invader of a weakened host still dogged him. His attempts to infect healthy animals were failures. Finally, he realised that if he was going to prove his hypothesis that *H. pylori* colonisation could occur without the presence of an ulcer in a healthy human host, he was going to have to use himself as a guinea pig.

In 1984, after undergoing tests to ensure he was ulcer and *H. pylori* free, he drank a cocktail of infected fluid which, as anticipated, left him with an extensive gastric infection. Whilst not conclusively proving that such an infection would always lead to ulcers, it did prove that there was no need for there to be a prior weakness or an ulcer for this bug to be able to colonise the stomach.

Marshall says they were now rubbing shoulders with some of the scientific and medical leaders of the world, and the rejections from those in Australia became less of an issue, but he still had no idea how hard the road ahead towards universal acceptance would be.

Those who personally knew Marshall and had been privy to his and Warren's research were supportive, but without formal recognition or international interest, their findings were at real risk of being ignored. Marshall decided the best way to gather support was to present his findings at conferences and face up to the questions and dissent of the audience.

"At one conference, I can remember almost leaping off the stage and wanting to throttle people who were making inane comments about the whole thing."

But by the early 1990s the tide of acceptance began to turn, and by 1992 Marshal could go to meetings and have 50/50 support for his work. He was regularly being invited to be a keynote speaker at conferences, which reflected well on Australia.

Finally, in 1994, the US National Health Institute declared the correct treatment for duodenal ulcers was the eradication of *H. pylori* using antibiotics.

Marshall says they always knew they would win the battle, but even so, 'victories' can be sorely delayed. With few other options, he said it was conferences that gave him exposure to a global audience, as well as exposure to certain pharmaceutical companies, which then provided funding for his future research. Over time, Marshall's attention has spread to diagnostics and the associated business side of his work. Conferences were important here, too, as they can play a huge part in industry by raising awareness of other technologies that are available, and providing opportunities to promote your work. Marshall believes conferences and exhibitions also provide a mechanism for the technology companies to expand, not just by meeting potential buyers' needs but also by developing potential global distribution channels.

For example, he said that when his own company was showcasing his diagnostic products at conferences, it wasn't the actual sales at the conference that were of greatest value, but the enormous mailing list they gained access to.

Another vitally important element of a good conference, according to Marshall, is good media management.

"If the conference gets its media ducks in a row it can gain huge exposure. Conferences need to have a media budget and local media should be encouraged to access these world leaders for stories whilst they're here visiting. Organisers should get the news crews out the day before the conference and have the coverage continue throughout."

He cites the practice in Japan, where conference organisers get a public speaker to talk to parliament about the proceedings, generating priceless publicity.

Marshall believes that, if conference media is planned correctly, organisers can utilise the publicity to provide multiple benefits for their cause or for the research and products being showcased. Again, he draws on his own experience:

"[In the 1980s] the Australian health care system was so good that people already had access to low cost care, and had little incentive to look for alternatives."

They believed what their doctors had told them; that their ulcer was a result of their genetics or their lifestyle, that they would just have to live with it, and that antacids were the best way to manage it. Of course, Marshall believed many of them had been misdiagnosed, and knew they were simply not aware of the alternative treatments being tested, but he had no legitimate or ethical way to formally access these people or get information to them about what he was doing because it was seen as somewhat unethical for scientists or medical researchers to directly use the media to attract publicity or attention. But by speaking at conferences about his discoveries and the trials he was conducting, reports often appeared in local media and before long his office would be inundated with people wanting to be involved.

He said similar levels of public or commercial interest could be generated when the media reports on new technologies being showcased at conferences. He recalled a news segment about tiny cameras that had been developed to travel down patients' throats, allowing specialists to see inside their gut. When patients then came to be treated, they would often demand what they had seen on TV. Essentially, he sees that, by using media effectively, conference organisers can reach much larger audiences than just those in attendance. In terms of medical and scientific conferences, this has the power to shape patients' understanding and desires, and it can actually fuel a medical market.

He added that sponsors and investors also feel they've received better value for their investment when there is significant media exposure associated with a conference.

In fact, in terms of the overall importance of conferences to the field of science and medicine, Marshall ranks them 8 out of 10.

"Scientific development would happen anyway, but new knowledge is terribly important and it's also important for your own career to be exposed to that new knowledge. Conferences give you access to material that's not going to be published for a year or two, so if you don't go to a conference at least once every two years you become out of touch and your ideas could be superseded."

Marshall believes it is vital that Australian researchers go to international conferences to become known, and that international conferences are hosted here so local issues can be discussed one-on-one. He believes there is much potential for conferences in Australia to attract those from Asia and Indonesia, particularly conferences held in Perth, although Perth is a more difficult destination for those travelling from Europe and the United States. Marshall also believes it is important that conference organisers attract good sponsors to subsidise costs, but the most important thing organisers need to do is generate interest, so that people are calling you, wanting to attend.

He says that if Australia wants to keep its home-grown scientists and make them world class, local conferences are vitally important, and young researchers in particular should be encouraged to attend.

"They provide a means to keep you connected to the world and give you access to new knowledge. Young researchers should try to do at least a poster presentation as well when they attend a conference, because anything, even if it's small, can go on a CV. It shows they are trying, and that they're a self-starter, and this can increase opportunities for jobs overseas.

"All of this provides exponential benefits as it links Australian research with world leaders, keeping them up to date and garnering international recognition, which will lead to a growth in those wanting to pursue research careers here in Australia."

Another very important benefit of conferences for Marshall is the personal connections and friendships that are made.

"Those friendships are invaluable, and provide an ongoing means of support. I remember people who came to my early conferences and now I forever owe them a favour because they supported me when my field was tiny and controversial."

Now Professor of Clinical Microbiology at The University of Western Australia and Director of the Marshall Centre for Infectious Diseases (Research and Training), Marshall has a string of awards including the Florey Medal, the Benjamin Franklin Medal for Life Science, the Order of Australia, the Keio Medical Science Prize, the Buchanan Medal and more. What started out in 1981 as little more than a possibility for a "nice little research paper" about a new strain of bacteria would one day earn Warren and Marshall the most coveted of scientific awards.

"Robin and I thought we had a chance at a Nobel, but years had gone by since our discoveries, and we hadn't won. Robin had retired, but we still always went down to the pub for fish and chips on the night of the big announcement.

"When we finally heard in 2005 that we'd won, there were mixed emotions. It was a bit like dying and going to heaven; once you get there what do you do?"

Clearly there is no single factor to be credited for this achievement, which has undoubtedly saved lives and diminished the suffering of millions of people throughout the world. Marshall's colourful, adventurous childhood with capable, loving parents stimulated a thirst for answers, gave him the practical knowledge he needed to find them, and nurtured in him the courage and risk-taking spirit he needed in order to stick to his convictions.

Timing and luck played their parts too, as did the encouragement and friendship of Warren, Skirrow and other important supporters along the way. But it is also clear that conferences played an extremely important part in the process. Conferences and seminars provided Marshall with the opportunity to publicly showcase his and Warren's work in front of receptive – and not so receptive – local and international audiences. For, it is highly likely that without that level of controversy, interest and support generated as a result of conferences, the weight of the opposition against them would have at best significantly delayed the development of the simple and cost-effective diagnostic tests and treatments for these infections or, at worst, like Freedberg, may have discouraged these Nobel Prize winning adventurers from continuing with their work at all.

THE **STORIES**

08

Ian Chubb

Advancing Scientific Education

In his five years as Australia's Chief Scientist, Professor Ian Chubb AC attended a staggering number of meetings, forums and conferences, delivering opening addresses, keynote speeches and important presentations at around 100 events each year. Those in his audiences listened with interest as he wove together recollections, facts and anecdotes that helped illustrate the messages he hoped to convey, and few would have imagined that the man at the front of the room was once so shy his legs shook uncontrollably as he struggled his way through the nightmare of public speaking.

Whilst Chubb acknowledges the importance of conferences generally, and the benefits that come from the linkages and connections they facilitate, his personal perspective and experience of conferences is quite different.

"I wasn't an academic researcher who enjoyed conferences," he confessed.

"There are some people I know who would go to the opening of a brown paper bag, but I wasn't one of those people and I could not easily mooch in to large groups of people or pursue the star around the room."

As a young researcher, he attended a two-week conference in America that struck him as being so ritualistic and contrived it left him with doubts about whether he was on the right path.

"During the day everything was formal, then during the night the stars from the American science circuit would go and get changed into jeans and polo shirts and sneakers and wherever they walked they would be attended by a number of PhD or Post Doctorate aspirants, because this was the way you connected. I looked at it and thought, 'well if that's what you have to do to advance, this is not for me.'"

Chubb was also terrified at the thought of speaking in front of a room filled with strangers.

"When I was at my first conference in my twenties and I stood up to speak about my work, I thought I was just going to fall over. Even a few years later at another conference presentation on my work, I remember standing up there thinking to myself ... 'well it's a good job my trousers are so loose they can't see how much my legs are shaking'. Somehow I survived it and now I

wander into a room and sometimes adlib for half an hour, but back then it was really quite difficult."

Apart from his fear of public speaking, Chubb also admits he's never been comfortable walking into a room filled with strangers waiting to hear him speak.

"I still find it very difficult to walk into a room of 20, 30, 50, 1000 people where I don't know anyone, and I'm not someone who easily works the room; who can just go up and start talking to people as if I've been there with them for the last four hours. There are people who are good at that. I know that. I appreciate their strengths and I appreciate that's one of my weaknesses."

Chubb says his love for all things science was sparked at the small school he attended in regional Victoria, where his one teacher constantly sent students outside to study leaves and insects, and then rewarded those who were naturally curious and competitive.

"If you were curious and competitive and did well over a month or so, you got a pencil with an eraser on the end. I was always curious and competitive, and I still am."

He worked part-time as a junior technician in a research lab whilst doing his undergraduate studies and then set off to discover what the rest of the world had to offer. He settled for a while in Belgium, where he was a Heymans Research Fellow at the University of Ghent, and despite his personal aversion to conferences, accepted they were part and parcel of his fellowship. This was also where he married his French language teacher, Claudette, and started a family.

Chubb says conferences back then were more about pure science, with very little of the business focus seen today.

"I attended conferences in my early years but they were mostly scientific conferences. My generation of scientists were brought up very fundamentally on science and we did research that may at the most be only peripherally engaged with any businesses. There were some exceptions but we weren't encouraged to go out and innovate and to think of ideas to commercialise

and do start-ups and all the rest; we were encouraged to do good science and the expectation was that we would end up academic scientists and that's what many of my generation did."

But for the present generation, he sees things have changed.

"Business is a big part of the conference audience now, whereas in my day if you had business involved it was to sponsor the morning tea or the afternoon drinks or something like that. It was a different attitude, the world's different."

As a result of a connection made at one of those early conferences, Chubb was offered a place on a research team at Oxford a few years later, and whilst there received his Master's Degree in science and arts and a PhD in philosophy.

Nearly a decade after leaving Australia, he returned in the late 1970s to take up an academic position at Flinders University. It was here that his work and teaching focused on the neurosciences, and over the next seven years, as well as his teaching, he established a highly successful and well-funded neuroscience research team and was chair of a number of important university and national research and grants committees.

By his own admission, a 'fairly impatient person', who thrived on challenge, Chubb still felt he had more to contribute, and after an evening in his backyard looking up at the stars, decided the time was right for him to move into the area of tertiary education management, direction and reform.

He progressed quickly through the ranks of university governance, serving as Deputy Vice Chancellor of the University of Wollongong from 1986–1990, Senior Deputy Vice-Chancellor at Monash University 1993–1995, Vice Chancellor of Flinders University 1995–2001 and Vice Chancellor of the Australian National University (ANU) 2001–2011.

In 2010, aged 67, Chubb naturally began toying with the idea of retirement and tendered his resignation from ANU to become effective in February 2011. But, as fate would have it, as the date approached, the then Chief Scientist for Australia, US-born physicist Penny Sackett, unexpectedly resigned from the position midway through her term. Within weeks of his 'retirement', Chubb was offered the top job (an 'easy transition to retirement,' he was told) and from his first day, worked tirelessly to ensure educators, policy-makers and the general public were made aware of the importance of science not only to our quality of life, but to our very survival.

And fan or no fan, one of his most frequently used tools for ensuring those messages reached a broad audience were the speeches he gave at conferences.

Given Chubb's nature, his experiences and his deeply rooted foundations in the facts and figures of fundamental science, it comes as no surprise that, when hypothesising about possible long-term outcomes of conferences or the extent to which they've impacted his own career or the opinions of those in his audiences, he would like further evidence.

"Well, I think the short answer is that I don't think they've been much influence on me personally, and as far as the audience goes, well, I don't know the answer to that question. I don't really think what I say changes those listening on the day, and many of them I won't ever see again, or they might be in the audience when I talk on some other topic but I don't go up to them and say 'Have you changed your mind on climate change?' or whatever, so I don't really know."

But he will go so far as to admit that the fact that he's often invited back to speak again indicates audiences are listening.

"I think the best illustration to some extent is that I get repeat invites. I give about 100 speeches a year to all sorts of groups and bodies and in order to accept 100 invitations I probably decline about 200 or 300 because I just can't fit them all in, so I guess that shows you have some influence on the way people think or at least that they want to hear what you've got to say."

And what he's had to say so eloquently over the past few years are his thoughts on things such as the decline of students enrolling in STEM subjects (science, technology, engineering and maths) at schools and universities, and what impact that might have upon Australia's future; how to engage students in the wonders of science; the growing importance of citizen science; the research priorities for our nation as we look to our future; and what new information science can offer as climate change continues to shift from a theoretical concept to a reality of life.

It seems those in his audiences were listening. The National STEM School Education Strategy, a comprehensive plan for science, technology, engineering and mathematics education in Australia, was released in December 2015. That same year, the Australian Government established its Science and Research Priorities, along with the corresponding Practical Research Challenges strategy, designed to increase investment of funds for scientific research in areas of immediate and critical importance to the country.

So, with Chubb's personal aversion to the pomp and ceremony of formal conferences and public speaking, what value, if any, does he feel they have in terms of knowledge dissemination or information sharing in his field?

Once again grounding himself on an evidence-based platform, he says the fact that so many conferences are still taking place around the world, and along similar lines to the way things were done 30 or 40 years ago, tells you they are of value.

"Whether it's just seeing people who work in your field and having the opportunity to talk to them off line, or whether you actually go to hear a particular lecture, I think there's some value in sitting in a room and listening to someone talk and looking at their slides."

But he suspects the big value of conferences lies in the connections made during breaks.

"When I was attending those earlier conferences there were a number of us of a similar age and stage of our careers, and sometimes working in fields that were quite close to each other (and even different fields), but you find people you like. I still have communications today with people I met during that period, and I think that happened in some cases not because I was particularly interested in or working in the same field as them but just because in the breaks you meet some people you find agreeable and that's important, especially for young people, even more so today than it was in my day.

"I think having a bunch of people you can talk to frankly and freely about life, how your career's developing, how hard it is to get a research grant, how you prepare your applications, how hard it is to get published somewhere, how hard the Vice Chancellor is on all young people ... doesn't support them... and how if only you could be Vice Chancellor at any age between 28 and 68 you'd doubtless change the world for the better ... All that stuff – they're important conversations to have and I think that one way you do that outside your immediate area is by going to large group meetings and conferences where you can meet and talk to people about all sorts of matters – including your science."

When Chubb was secretary of the Australasian Neuroscience Society Inc. he tried to ensure their conferences weren't too formally structured, leaving plenty of time for casual conversations and the formation of networks so people could meet people.

"We tried to organise things around the informal connections that you make at lunch or morning tea or over a drink or a dinner or whatever it might be. We organised our conferences on a reasonably informal basis, but they were also fairly small. They're a lot bigger now and once they get big the whole picture changes."

Chubb believes that young researchers, or those starting out in their careers can benefit most from conferences, particularly in terms of their personal growth and career-enhancing opportunities. He says this was why he made efforts during his time at ANU to set aside additional funding to send young people to conferences, thereby improving not only their learning but also their future employment prospects.

"It's relatively easy to get enrolled in a PhD in Australia these days, and in some ways some of these students are exploited because they're cheap labour and they do research and it results in publications, which all help the income of the university or even its international ranking, whatever that means."

Chubb says there are around 60 000 registered Higher Degree research students in Australia today, and the reality is that only a very small proportion will end up in an academic career.

"Still, these students remain hopeful, so they do a Post Doc and then have to depend on someone else to get a research grant to fund them for another 3 years or so, and then they have to apply again and they don't find out until December whether they've still got a job in January. That whole area has become a sad aspect of the development of our sector. These students need to be able to go to conferences to talk to people about their work, to meet people, and to meet some of the elder statesmen, because they might well need their support at some point when they go for a job or another post doc or whatever [it] may be."

He believes such students should be more appropriately resourced and supported as they work towards their goals.

"I think we should be looking after these people much better than we do. Traditionally, we've just said, well here's a PhD scholarship and here is some money for your PhD supervisor – but it's not good enough and I think this is an issue that needs to be corrected."

If he was organising conferences now, he says he would try to do things along the line of the 'flipped classroom', where there would be more of a focus on shared discussion than talking 'at' those in the audience.

"I'd get the key information out to everyone beforehand, and then I'd gather together a group of people and I'd just turn it into a discussion session. Someone might still come up to you in the coffee break and say they didn't understand Table Two and that's ok and that would continue to be a part of it, but the reality is what you need to do is to have the person stand up in the middle of the group, in front of a number of others and engage with them all – not, I repeat, talk at them all.

"It would be a much more useful way of doing it compared to saying 'well, I'm going to talk to you for at least 12.5 of my allotted time and we'll have 2.5 minutes for questions' and then someone rings a bell and says 'right, its coffee time now, stop.'"

He admits such a format would be difficult at large conferences, with thousands of attendees, but even here he believes it could be done with some of the breakouts.

"If, for example, there are four papers connected with a particular session ... distribute them beforehand ... and for an hour (if there were four of them) run a dicussion about the work described in those papers rather than something as regimented as a speech.

"And I'd do that if I were still teaching too. I think giving a lecture to 400 is one way of doing things, but it's the old way of doing things. Instead, you might divide them up into a couple of groups and say, well here is all you need to know to come to this meeting to discuss the evidence or whatever it is, these principals, these theories etc. and have a discussion."

Always thinking deeply, Chubb gave a measured response when asked where conferences sat on a scale of 1 to 10 in terms of the importance they played in knowledge diffusion in the field of science, concluding instead that it was dependent upon how international one's particular area of research was.

"Well, if you're working on the Australian Education system, then you would have one answer to that question, but if your area of expertise was the study of rocks near Alice Springs you'd have a slightly different answer, and if you're working in a field like climate change you would have an entirely different response again.

"If I were a climate scientist, conferences would be very important because it's the one opportunity to bring people from all around the world together to have face-to-face discussion drawing on evidence from all their different disciplines. I mean, you can read what they do when they publish it in journals – but conferences are really important if you want to understand what's behind what they've written.

"I think conferences are important to all fields, but the importance varies, and putting them somewhere on a scale is difficult because it depends on how big and how widely diffused your field of research is."

Receiving an Order of Australia in 2006, and being named ACT Australian of the Year in 2011 for extensive service to Australian tertiary education, Chubb has a long list of appointments and awards, and yet proudly acknowledges that his greatest achievement is his family. With his forthright, honest nature and his intelligence and drive, he's managed to bundle three successful careers into a single happy life; and as he once again contemplates his future, staring up at the night sky from his suburban backyard, one cannot help but wonder what distant mountain he is next planning to climb.

THE **STORIES**

09

Brian Schmidt

Proving That The Universe Is Speeding Up

Nobel Prize winning astrophysicist, and newly appointed Vice-Chancellor of the Australian National University (ANU), Brian Schmidt says conferences have been an invaluable part of his life's work; work that has radically reshaped our understanding of how the universe functions and where it may be headed.

"Astronomy without conferences would mean a bunch of little people working on things without understanding what everyone else in the world was working on, so they are absolutely core to what we all do."

What Schmidt and his fellow researchers have 'done' to earn them the Nobel Prize in Physics was to challenge and disprove one of the most basic assumptions upon which their field of science had been based.

Thanks largely to Einstein's 1915 theories on the forces of gravity, there has been general consensus that, although the universe is still expanding, its rate of expansion is slowing, perhaps for eternity, or perhaps eventually stopping and then reversing – into something of a pre-'big-bang' cosmic arrangement.

But in 1994 a handful of cosmic scientists began tracking and recording massive exploding stars called supernovae and soon found themselves trying to make sense of unanticipated research findings that challenged this long-held assumption of a decelerating universe.

American born, but a self-proclaimed and now official Australian, Schmidt credits Australia's approach to science and discovery for giving him the freedom to explore and expand upon what their research was telling them, but admits even he doubted the validity of their initial findings because they went against all he'd previously been taught to be true.

"When we first started seeing the data (more than 3 years after embarking on the experiment), I remember just thinking, 'Oh jeez, we've made a mistake. What have we done wrong?'"

Over the next several months, Schmidt, who led the international collaboration, High-Z Supernova Search Team, worked with Dr Adam Riess from the Space Telescope Science Institute in the US, checking and rechecking every step they'd taken, searching for the source of their error, but every time the conclusion was the same: the distant exploding stars were showing that the universe was speeding up, rather than slowing down.

In other words, the speed at which our universe was expanding was actually increasing over time – not decreasing – as had previously been assumed.

Their discovery of the accelerating universe was of such significance that in 2011 Schmidt and Riess, and Saul Perlmutter (who led a rival US team that had reached the same conclusion as Schmidt's team in 1998), were jointly awarded the Nobel Prize in Physics. It was one of the few times the prize had gone to astronomers, and according to National Geographic, was perhaps the most important scientific discovery of the last quarter of the 20th century; the most important of the previous quarter century being the discovery of DNA.

So why is this new information so important, and how does it help us into the future?

Essentially, apart from resolving a lot of the previous problems of cosmology and giving clearer, more accurate directions for future research, the observations led scientists to ask what was causing the acceleration, and hence laid the groundwork for the discovery of 'dark energy' – a previously undetected form of matter with very low density.

Difficult to measure or validate in laboratory testing, there are two leading models that explain dark energy, but both agree that the common characteristic is that it must have negative pressure, and that it acts upon itself in a repulsive manner.

In simple terms, it is this negative pressure that has gravity pushing this energy (which pervades all of space) apart at an ever increasing rate over time.

And whilst these discoveries are only the first step in predicting what our universe's final outcome might be, these scientists have at least set us on a path of greater understanding and uncovered a previously unseen force that is already determining the fate of distant celestial giants.

Brian Schmidt was born in Montana in 1967, the only child of parents just out of their teens. He developed a love of science whilst pottering in the lab and collecting specimens in the wild with his father, who was working on his PhD as a fisheries biologist. From his mother, a champion debater with qualifications in speech and communications, he learned how to move and motivate others with words. The young family shifted house constantly as he grew, and by 14 he had called 13 different places home, which gave him confidence in new situations and taught him how to easily make friends.

Initially leaning towards a career in meteorology, he shifted to astronomy after a school placement at a weather bureau left him disappointed. Bored with the party scene as an undergrad at the University of Arizona, he took on extra subjects (doing two degrees in the time most people take to do one), conducted his own research projects on the side, and still had time at his disposal to pursue his love of bread and pastry making. After graduating with great academic results, he moved to Harvard, where he did a Masters and then a PhD in Astronomy, and says it was only then that he really began to do serious science.

It was also then that he was introduced to conferences, and quickly came to understand the important role they could play in his life.

"My adviser, Robert Kirshner, came up to me in 1990 and said, 'You need to go to this conference in Les Houches, France' – in the middle of the French Alps – I looked at him and said I didn't have enough money to go, but he said, 'Oh no, no, I'll pay. You'll go there and you'll learn and you'll do stuff.'"

Whilst at Les Houches, Schmidt had the opportunity to meet experts in his field and make important connections with other researchers working on similar projects. One such connection was with a student from Chile, who was being supervised at the time by renowned US (and Chilean-based) astronomer, Nicholas Suntzeff.

"He invited me to visit him, so about a year later I went off to Chile for six weeks. I became very good friends with Nick while I was there, and after that I visited them on a regular basis and of course we'd meet up at conferences and things along the way, so it just became a very close relationship.

"It was my first conference experience, and to this day, one of the best. It was amazing, and brought me in contact with all of the leaders of the field and really those leaders – those relationships persist to this day."

He says conferences are the sites where you really find out what's going on in astronomy; what's leading us, what's important, where ideas mix.

"Science is so international; you have to travel. The internet is not perfect. You cannot spend weeks in conferences with people via the phone; it just doesn't work. You have to travel if you're going to communicate ideas. And so as a scientist you get to travel. I remember being overwhelmed at being able to do that."

Schmidt says Suntzeff became one of his mentors, and in 1994 they co-founded the High-Z (Z means redshift) Supernova Search Team, which led to the Nobel Prize.

Another important connection established while at Harvard was with Australian economics PhD candidate Jenny Gordon, whom he married in 1992. One rule they agreed upon was that they both needed to find work in the same city – so when Brian was offered a three-year position at Mt Stromlo at the Australian National University in Canberra, Jenny (today an economist with the Australian Productivity Commission) jumped at one of the many opportunities that Canberra afforded her.

But the first Australian to win a Nobel Prize for Physics in nearly 100 years, and now Vice-Chancellor at ANU, says he came close to leaving the field altogether in 1997: his post coming to an end, Schmidt applied for a research fellowship, but only succeeded in achieving fourth in line for the position.

"It was looking like I might have to return to the States for work or, more likely, do something else, but then, interestingly, the other three people who'd been ranked ahead of me turned it down, so they gave it to me! It was very soon after that I helped discover the accelerating universe, and so I guess my career was pretty well solidified from there on."

Schmidt says it's the personal interactions that occur at conferences that are the most important element, and one which technology can't provide.

"You might be able to support interactions with other people with technology one-on-one or even group-to-group, but you can't have 2 000 people or even 200 people show up on a video link. I've done those and they're terrible! They've really been bad."

He says technology has a place for supporting ongoing collaboration, but only once a personal relationship has been established in a setting such as a conference.

"What I find is if I build a relationship with someone in person at a conference, then I can follow it up with Skype or hopefully a TelePresence-like technology that's a bit better, and that way, you can maintain that relationship. But you do need to meet people in person that you're working with, in my opinion, every year or so, and then you can have those regular meetings by video."

He also believes one's potential to learn from attending a conference is much greater than that which can occur from reading research papers.

"When you read papers, it's dry, and it's hard to separate out the interesting bits from the non-interesting bits. They tend to be single things without a lot of reference to everything else. But at conferences, people are putting their latest work into context with everything that everyone else is doing, so you can really get a snapshot of the field as it is at that time, in a way that you just don't get from any other avenue."

And for students trying to get their head around new and complex concepts, Schmidt believes conferences are even more valuable in terms of their ability to make content stick.

"If you've got a student, and you tell them to read a million articles, maybe one per cent will be useful for them.

"But if you send them to a conference, then they get an instant snapshot of where the whole field is, which is much more useful."

Schmidt, who attends many conferences across the world each year and hosts quite a few in Sydney with his own team, says he comes away from most conferences with a list of new ideas or questions to investigate.

"To be honest, many of my ideas come from attending conferences and I just go out with a list of things I need to think about."

In fact, Schmidt estimates an astounding 75 per cent of all research papers he's written have one way or another come out of a conference.

He says that, whilst the concept of an accelerated universe wasn't a specific idea gleaned from a conference, the collaborations he established with the people he met at conferences, as well as some of the applications he has used in the projects, have definitely made a huge contribution.

"Some of the gamma ray burst stuff that I've done, which are the biggest explosions in the universe, came from a conference I attended.

"I realised I could develop some of the technology they were using, combine it with a telescope we had here in Australia, and use some of the software from the accelerating universe project to look for transient objects quickly, so the conference jump-started that research, and that's probably the second biggest thing I've done in my career."

He says seeing technology used by others at conferences can open up windows in your mind as you imagine the applications you can find for it in your own area of research.

"You'll see someone using a new piece of equipment somewhere in the world, and you'll realize you'd be able to use it here.

"At the moment we're looking at [a] new type of imager much stronger than ours which came specifically from talking to someone at a conference about how it could be used. It was a new technology, a new infrared sensor technology that can essentially take images at many hundreds of times per second, which is a new thing we just weren't able to do in the past.

"Now, thanks to the conference, we know about it and want to bring it to Australia.

"It's kind of hard to pick examples about where and how conferences have helped, because they're just such an important part of literally everything we do."

So, for Schmidt, whose theory of an accelerating universe brought him and his team a place in the record books and international acclaim, and whose discoveries have focused the astronomical community upon completely new horizons, just how important have conferences been – not only to his own career but to the inspiration, creation and diffusion of ideas and knowledge throughout the scientific community?

"Well, I think they're pretty close to ten out of ten," he insists.

"I mean, without conferences, productivity would dramatically drop, so to me, they're pretty much essential. And as far as my own career goes, that first conference I went to in France was such a special moment, and an amazing opportunity because it just set the stage for my whole career, and you only get one of those in your life ... [It's] why I always make sure that my students are able to go to them. It's one of the things I prioritize over almost anything else."

THE **STORIES**

10

Linda Burney

Indigenous Educational Reform

In August 2016, when Linda Burney stood to deliver her maiden speech as the first Indigenous woman elected to the Australian House of Representatives, she touched hearts and minds across the country, and in fact the world, as she told of the journey travelled to bring her to that day.

From beginnings that would have left others broken and angry, Burney used the challenges and adversity she faced as a child to strengthen her spirit and fire a determination to bring about positive change in terms of how Indigenous people lived, were treated and perceived in Australian society.

Given up by her unmarried white mother at birth, and not knowing her Indigenous father until adulthood, Burney credits elderly Scottish-born Letitia and Billy Laing for making her the person she is today. Despite the racism and intolerance directed towards Indigenous people inherent in Australian society at the time, the Laings bravely became foster parents to the tiny baby and passed on to her their own values of courage, tolerance, wisdom and respect for others.

"I think I was very lucky to be raised by my great aunt and uncle who are brother and sister, who developed in me a great love of learning and reading.

"I've also had the great fortune in my life to have both Aboriginal and non-Aboriginal people around me that have supported me and allowed me to rest on their shoulders, and they've given me a wonderful set of principles to live my life by."

It is those principles which have seen Burney already achieve well beyond the expectations many from her home town of Whitton had for her as a child, and which some believe may carry her one day to the highest office in the country. Previous President of the NSW Aboriginal Education Consultative Group (AECG), a member of the Board of Studies and previous National President of the Australian Labor Party 2008–2009, Burney is now the Federal Member for Barton and shadow Federal Minister for Human Services, but she says it's her achievements in terms of educational reform, not politics, of which she is most proud.

"I think my most important contribution thus far is probably the extensive work I did in the education arena, in particular the curriculum work. I was President of the NSW Aboriginal Education Consultative Group (AECG) and a member of the Board of Studies for a very long time, so I had enormous influence on curriculum development. I also led the policy debate for many years both in NSW and nationally on ways to incorporate Aboriginal studies into the curriculum, and also discussion on things like Aboriginal conditions, employment, education and social rights."

Burney says one of the most important elements of the overall reform strategy was the Aboriginal Educational Conferences of the 1990s.

"The conferences were critical!"

According to Burney, the real value of the conferences lay in the way they enabled organisers to bring different people with different perspectives together in discussion.

"It's as simple as that: they put people together.

"Certainly there was a very definite political element to the conferences and participants were always mindful their overall objective was to bring about policy change, but it was the way the conferences brought everyone together to establish common goals that helped us achieve the level of success which we did.

"We had the involvement of Aboriginal and non-Aboriginal people and we all knew we were there working for a common cause."

Burney says the conferences were always about two things: equitable outcomes for Aboriginal children, and Aboriginal studies and truth-telling for all children.

"Firstly we needed to make sure Aboriginal kids were getting literacy and numeracy education and all those sorts of things, but secondly there was the fact that for me, going to school in the 70's, the version of history we learned about Aboriginal people was that they were non-existent or if the story was told in schools at all, it was very biased.

"If you read the statement that I often make of my experience as a 13 year old kid being told in class that your people were savages and they were the closest examples we had to stone-aged man, well they were some of the moments in my life that led me to be an educator.

"The respect and admiration that non-Aboriginal youth have for indigenous Aboriginal people today is much greater than it was 40 years ago, and that's all come about through the curriculum work I've been involved in."

As well as the ongoing conferences, the NSW Aboriginal Education Consultative Group held an AGM each year which lasted for three or four days.

"Of course we would look at the organisation's constitution and elect office bearers and everything, but we would also have representatives from the Department of Education there to inform and listen, and other agencies such as TAFE would come in to give reports. This helped significantly because those groups were then accountable to the AECG for what they were doing in terms of Aboriginal education, so it was absolutely setting the agenda for the future.

"Having those agencies come back and report annually [at conferences] also really helped us to monitor how things were going."

In addition to evaluating activities and setting the agenda, Burney said conferences also played a role in the bigger picture of reform for Aboriginal people that began in the 1980s.

"In those earlier days there were conferences that were just for Aboriginal people, where we started striking out and demanding self-determination and to be listened to."

Then, in the middle to latter part of the reconciliation process, when John Howard was winding back Native Title policy, Burney was involved in the organisation of the 1997 Australian Reconciliation Convention in Melbourne.

"That was a ground-breaking conference. We had international speakers and brought 2 000 people together to talk about reconciliation, and we really set the direction for where we wanted to go.

"That was probably the stand-out conference for me."

When she was Director General, NSW Department of Aboriginal Affairs, she also used conferences to bring together elders from different Aboriginal settlements across the state.

"Those conferences were absolutely brilliant, and it's a crying shame that they've not been continued. I brought together for the first time, in a very long time, Aboriginal elders from across NSW and it was powerful.

"It was important in terms of culture, in terms of giving elders the status and respect they deserve, and we set the agenda for a whole range of social justice areas, like juvenile justice, education, and more. Those discussions then informed debates in other areas, such as what was ethical, what wasn't ethical, Aboriginal political representation, Aboriginal languages, and the judiciary. What was important about those conferences was that we were able to look at future directions from the elders' perspectives."

Burney says that, again, these conferences were critical in achieving the outcomes for Aboriginal people being seen today.

"What happened at those conferences was extraordinary. We took instruction from the elders and set parameters for other discussions going forward, particularly in terms of NSW."

But she adds that, apart from the social justice and reform outcomes, the conferences were a way of acknowledging the important role the elders played within their culture.

"Apart from anything else, it was a good way to recognise what these people had done, and to simply bring them together. It doesn't always have to be about setting an agenda or achieving massive outcomes. This was also about recognising and respecting the wisdom of the elders and giving them a chance to be together to reinforce their strength or resilience, and to just talk about whatever they wanted to talk about."

Importantly, she said opportunities to gather and talk in such settings often led to outcomes in and of themselves, and often in ways that may never be known.

"Meetings and conferences can set the long and short term goals and priorities, so you know what you have to do going forward, but they can be just as important for the networking and support opportunities they provide.

"For example, the AGMs of the AECG were fundamentally a network of regional and local volunteer groups, and so to bring those people together annually was really important for exchanging ideas and for being able to say, 'look you know – you're not the only one out there feeling this way' or 'Yes, it's hard, but this is what we did to resolve that situation in our area – it may not work in your area but maybe it will.'"

With her political career gathering momentum, Burney believes conferences may have a part to play in the resolution of other major issues, such as terrorism and abuse or deaths in custody.

"Absolutely they [conferences] can play a part in those types of issues. I don't believe – even with the advent of social media and other technologies like video conferencing or teleconferences – that anything can replace people sitting down together in a room, over dinner, over a drink, over a discussion in a workshop.

"You just can't see the body language.

"Not only do conferences have the face-to-face, sitting down talking in the formal session, but importantly there's also the social setting around a conference where people can really thrash out issues, set priorities and collaborate. You just need to be able to see people and to see how they're reacting in order to judge how the conversation is going. There is nothing that can replace that face-to-face dialogue."

She believes that with the range of settings usually offered at a conference there is flexibility to use different strategies to achieve your objectives.

"If you start a conversation and it doesn't go well, you know you can pick it up again that afternoon or in a social setting. Likewise, if you try something in the conference and it's not working out, you have the capacity to change direction, to change the agenda, to mould it around what the needs are of the people that are there.

"You can have new people come in, you get stimulation, you get presentations, you get ideas ... and apart from that they're bloody good fun sometimes.

"It's called creating friends and relationships."

With the successful conference outcomes Burney herself has experienced, she believes they will continue to be an important part of the way forward. And she believes the range of benefits that result from a well-run conference far outweigh the costs.

"It seems to me there's been this kind of attitude of 'Oh, it's too expensive ... they're just talkfests' ... but I don't see conferences that way at all. If they are properly run, and well structured, the values are enormous. If they're not run well, then maybe they're just talkfests ... But good conferences have tangible benefits and outcomes. I've organised so many of them, and they're bloody hard work, so you don't do it because you want a good time and a talkfest."

Burney says the logistics of organising a conference are crucial.

"You need to plan everything down to what cheese is going to be on the cheese platter is my approach. You make sure you have a long lead-in time and you have to get the right people there. Most importantly, you have to make sure your purpose is absolutely clear, that everyone knows why they're there, and that your facilitators are fantastic."

With the increased focus on financial accountability, Burney worries that the value of conferences may be overlooked.

"I suspect that as money becomes tighter and tighter, the one thing that will go by the wayside is gatherings of people."

And whilst conferences may have the potential to engage the wider community in important issues and influence social policy, Burney says it depends in many ways upon the type and level of media and political exposure that has been generated.

"Engaging in the political process was crucial in getting the outcomes we did, particularly when it came to influencing social policy. One of the things we always did, particularly through the NSW AECG and the National AECG was invite the minister of the day [to] come and speak. We would also get other ministers from various portfolio areas because that would help raise the status and set the agenda.

"Having the minister come and face up to a whole group of people was always very powerful and very useful, because not only did you get an understanding of what they thought was important – but they also got an understanding of what you thought was important."

Burney adds that while involving politicians in conferences can have an impact on social reform, shifts in public opinion can only occur if the messages created are allowed to reach the wider community.

"Conferences can shape social policy and political discourse, but I'm not sure how successful they are in shaping public opinion, because the public still needs to get access to what's talked about at that conference. Basically it just depends on what the conference has organised in terms of getting the messages out there."

In summing up, Burney rates the importance of conferences for stimulating innovation a 9 out of 10, and gives them a healthy 8 out of 10 in terms of their contribution to knowledge sharing.

She also believes that, despite advances in technologies and communications, well-organised and resourced conferences with clear agendas and purpose will continue to be one of the most important tools available to those seeking to bring about social change.

"New media is not going to replace the value of people physically coming together ... the role that they play in society is that they bring people together, they set agendas and they set goals for various organisations – including government – to attain."

THE **INSIGHTS**

Long Tail Insights

There is growing evidence that many of the important innovations, significant discoveries and positive shifts in social practice and reform we benefit from today have arisen as a direct result of discussions, ideas and relationships initiated at conferences.

Life-saving medical breakthroughs, applications for new technologies and key strategies to guide our social development are increasingly linked to concepts and connections forged in conference environments, and those at the forefront of our quest to unlock the secrets of our universe believe conferences are a unique and vitally important tool which significantly enhances knowledge sharing and the generation of new ideas.

The idea for this book arose from three areas: our personal observations and experience of conferences, findings from our previous research, and our curiosity as researchers. What we have found is a collection of stories that lingers with us because of its ability to inspire. But more than this, we hope that readers will relate to the experiences shared, the business events industry will learn from these accounts and improve practices, and academics will ask their own questions and use this collection of stories to guide teaching activities and student learning. Thus, we hope that diverse readers will draw on the stories and use them in ways that meet their particular needs.

As we explained in the Introduction, we wanted to gain insights into the long tail of conferences and how moments of serendipity and innovation are sparked at such events. Human behaviour is complex, so it is only through stories such as these that we are able to find some clarity around how benefits can arise both during the conference and many years later.

This final chapter presents reflections at multiple levels – for students, researchers and practitioners looking to advance their knowledge and understanding of this industry sector, as well as providing a convenient summary.

Six themes have been drawn from these stories: creating networks, collaborations, partnerships and support; discussion, debate, stimulation, ideas and innovation; attracting funding, trade and investment; influencing public perceptions and policy and driving social change; personal growth, knowledge and learning; and lessons for industry. In distilling the themes, the reader may be stimulated to add their own perspectives, to elucidate their own insights, and to consider research that is required in the future. These themes have highlighted the complexity of conferences, which has led us to consider what a conference business model may look like given our new understanding.

This chapter concludes by suggesting areas for further research.

Creating Networks, Collaborations, Partnerships And Support

One of the strongest themes to arise from the stories is that a conference is an avenue for fostering networks – whether established or new. Networks were wide ranging and included: peer colleagues and researchers; clinicians; local enterprises; government agencies; various community groups and representatives; universities; non-profit associations; research funding agencies; consultants; suppliers; accreditation bodies; media; and customers.

Networks, collaborations, partnerships and support arose in a number of ways. For Dr Pia Winberg, these networks were interdisciplinary. She was able to connect with economists, investors and business people outside of her field of research – connections that proved instrumental to the development of her seaweed business. For others, interdisciplinary networks led to innovation from 'a cross-fertilization of ideas' that created new projects and research directions. Professor Chubb believed that networks were advantageous for his career enhancement and personal growth as an early-career researcher.

Similar sentiments were echoed by Professors Schmidt, Green and Frazer. Moreover, Professors Schmidt and Frazer referred to a 'multiplier effect'. Networking at conferences, they said, led to further networking post-conference, taking in a wider group of people, 'visiting contacts who introduce one to other people', whom they otherwise may not have met. Friendships built from these networks were highly valued for their pivotal role in providing much needed intellectual support, for which Professor Marshall is forever thankful – 'they supported me when my field was tiny and controversial', and Linda Burney felt they were crucial 'for building a sense of community'.

Discussion, Debate, Stimulation, Ideas And Innovation

As Foley, Edwards and Schlenker (2014) have previously demonstrated, within the social contexts of conferences, 'the sharing of knowledge and creative ideas occur and common meanings are developed through the interactions' (p. 28). It is a sentiment that is reinforced in the stories in this book. Conferences bring different people with different perspectives together to discuss and debate, which leads to the generation of new ideas and innovations. Burney felt that such face-to-face interactions led to conflict resolution and brought about social change; in part, because people's body language and reactions could be evaluated and responded to. For her, in these environments, people show respect by giving people an opportunity to voice their views.

Sometimes discussions can become heated and controversial, but for Dr Winberg it is important for the emotional aspects of an issue to be aired, as simply reading a scientific article means the information is restricted, factual and disconnected from lived experiences. Indeed, according to Professor Bowtell, open discussions enable culturally sensitive issues to be debated and for the realities of the situation to be made publicly known. In addition, the learning potential is greater because conferences provide an opportunity to get a snapshot of the field as it is at that time and students can 'get their head around new and complex concepts' in a meaningful way, as Professor Brian Schmidt asserted. Professor Green notes that conferences play a vital role in getting advice, learning how others are working, and learning about areas other than one's field.

For Professor Bowtell and Ms Burney conferences provide a focal point that can bring together different groups, many of whom have very different perspectives, and this leads to new ways of tackling problems and challenges. In Professor Calma's words, at conferences people are talking about 'the issues that matter', which can then lead to 'thought leadership'. In other words, 'discoveries are made by the exploitation of serendipitous opportunities by persons already primed to appreciate their significance' (Ziman 2002, p. 217). These long tail stories help us to appreciate how conferences lead to innovation by fertilising ideas, challenging previous thinking and driving new thinking.

With the knowledge that conferences generate inspiring ideas, Professor Schmidt attends conferences with a list of things he needs to think about, and looks for ideas that can assist him with future research and publications. While conferences stimulate the flow of technology, knowledge, values and ideas across borders, individuals will of course be affected differently and will take away from a conference that which is most important to them.

Attracting Funding, Trade And Investment

Research funding is highly competitive between individuals, research groups, research centres and universities. However, the stories here demonstrate that conferences can drive access to funding sources and create inducement for funding investment. Professor Green has been successful in securing international research funding, including from industry, by meeting and showcasing work at international conferences, and by using conference contacts to demonstrate collaboration for funding applications.

Dr Winberg has found conferences helpful in generating funding for research and development, and a formalised program of research was initiated as a direct result of conference attendance. Similar to Professor Calma, she has also had success with bringing business interests and researchers from industry together. She has done so by using conferences to test products for new medical applications, and has taken the opportunity to talk to investors and venture capitalists. She firmly believes that the rigour of conferences enables the participant to 'gain credibility'. For others, such as Professor Marshall, funding arising from conferences has enabled him to continue important medical trials. These opportunities may have arisen also as a result of the positive media generated.

Influencing Public Perceptions And Policy And Driving Social Change

A common thread through all the stories is the ability of conferences to influence public and media perceptions. According to Professor Marshall, if the "conference gets its media ducks in a row it can gain huge exposure". He gave the example of conferences in Japan inviting renowned experts to address the Japanese parliament, thereby getting the conference focus right into the heart of the policy-making arena. Similarly, Professor Bowtell stated that international and national policy on the treatment of AIDS was developed in response to conference presentations. Professor Marshall found conferences to be the driving force behind attracting people to participate in his clinical trials – a direct result of media reports which covered the research he presented at conferences. And Professor Tom Calma believes that key drivers behind the social and political shifts that have occurred for Indigenous Australians have arisen from conferences.

Personal Growth, Knowledge And Learning

Von Hippel (2005, p. 77) said that knowledge must be dispersed to others who can also benefit, for 'if user innovations are not diffused, multiple users with very similar needs will have to invest to (re)develop very similar innovations, which would be a poor use of resources from the social welfare point of view'. Conferences are very efficient at this task. According to Professor Marshall, conferences provide 'access to material that's not going to be published for a year or two ... if you don't go to a conference at least once every two years you become out of touch and your ideas could be superseded'. It is the ability of conferences to showcase the very latest technologies, instruments and knowledge that makes them superior to other methods of information sharing, enabling attendees to stay 'one step ahead in their thinking'.

Repeatedly, interviewees spoke of how conferences foster education and enable deeper learning. Attendees have access to works not yet published, learn from others beyond the education sector, and bridge knowledge gaps. These benefits lead to practical and theoretical outcomes, rapid transmission of solutions, and important changes in an individual's behaviour. Time and again interviewees spoke of the importance of going to conferences at the beginning of one's career, particularly as a young or emerging academic. As Dr Winberg said, 'they [early career academics] can learn more quickly how to contribute constructively and confidently to the conversations as their careers develop'.

The importance of knowledge sharing was highlighted by Professor Schmidt who said that without conferences it would mean that there would be 'a bunch of little people working on things without understanding what everyone else in the world was working on'.

Conferences enable attendees to increase their international credibility and reputation. Dr Winberg pointed out that conferences helped her to 'become internationally recognised as someone with expertise in this field of research'. Hosting conferences can be hard work, but the favourable impression made in the minds of attendees and the increased international standing and awareness of local research make it all worthwhile.

For Professor Calma, conferences were the catalyst for assisting indigenous people to be involved in managing their own education and providing steps to real change. Finally, conferences can assist people to step outside of their comfort zone and address areas that require personal and professional development, allowing them to reach their full potential.

The Long Tail Outcomes Summarised

The 10 stories demonstrate that conferences are shared social contexts which take people away from their established routines. Within this social context, knowledge and ideas are shared and common goals are developed through such interactions. It is not surprising then that these stories demonstrate a direct connection between the staging of conferences and an extensive range of benefits and outcomes beyond the tourism spend.

In previous work we have argued that the benefits and outcomes have impact in five broad areas: intrinsic, practice, social, economic and attitudinal (Edwards et al. 2011). As indicated in Table 1, overleaf, the legacies are not mutually exclusive – a benefit or outcome may have multiple legacies.

Intrinsic legacies are the personal outcomes delegates gain to develop their knowledge and skills. In the collaborative environment of the business event they are able to express and share their knowledge, skills and practices with a broad range of people including peers, colleagues, and others who may come from industry, government and not-for-profit organisations. Related to this are social legacies, which represent the camaraderie that develops around the conference, the appeal of engaging with other like-minded people, the relationships that are enhanced and developed, and the broader benefits that accrue to the communities in which the conference is held. Business events develop a social space that is important as it facilitates and reinforces social interaction and, in turn, influences the effectiveness of collaborative learning. Tacit knowledge can be spread through informal interactions with current and new colleagues.

Professional and practice legacies result from the skills and knowledge that delegates gain – such as attaining new insights, learning surgical techniques, sharing new ideas and identifying solutions to solving problems – being directly integrated into their professional practices and organisations. Professional legacies also arise for the delegate from gaining business partners, building research networks and obtaining knowledge that can solve research and business problems.

Attitudinal legacies arise from the reactions of delegates to their experiences at the conference, and from governments, the private sector and individuals who become aware of important issues that are communicated through the international and local media.

Economic legacies are realised as social networks affect the flow and the quality of information. Moving in different circles from one's own group connects people to a wider world and therefore any new acquaintances can be better sources of information as delegates go beyond what their own group knows. As conferences are intense periods during which social interaction is fostered, they lead to benefits and outcomes that have both intangible and tangible economic effects, such as building knowledge and capabilities, identifying business partners, improved workforce practices, better education, new investments, enhanced funding and better industry sector policies.

TABLE 1 BENEFIT AND OUTCOME LEGACIES ARISING FROM BUSINESS EVENTS

INTRINSIC

PROFESSIONAL PRACTICE

DURING EVENT	New ideas & 'aha' moments	New knowledge & skills
	Deep learning	Access to new technologies
	New/enhanced relationships	International standing
	Exposure to latest advancements	Cross cultural awareness
	Intellectual support	
POST EVENT	Expanded networks	Research collaborations
	Energy & momentum	Advanced medical trials
	Holistic understanding of the field	Knowledge/skill/technologies in workplaces
		Thought leadership
LONG TAIL	Communities of friendship & practice	Multiplier effect of knowledge & skills crossing organisational borders
	Enhanced careers	Organisational innovation
	Mastery of field	
	Future research	

Benefits to delegates & their workplaces

ATTITUDINAL

ECONOMIC

ATTITUDINAL	ECONOMIC
Media/publicity	Tourism contribution
Enhanced destination reputation	Academia & industry partnerships/investment
Making science relevant	
Influence on public perception	
Energised industry sectors	New/enhanced avenues of investment & trade
Raised awareness of sector	Community benefit from enhanced business practice
Government/community support	
Positive social change	Industry innovation
Policy development	Product development
	Medical breakthroughs
	Scientific discovery
	Thriving economies

Benefits to communities, industry sectors & economies

Lessons For Industry

Because of their diversity and richness, these stories provide practical tips for practitioners engaged in staging conferences.

Academics and practitioners are aware that no one person has sufficient knowledge to create the innovations that are required to compete globally. Conferences facilitate conversations across individuals and groups who may not normally come together. They provide a temporal and spatial mechanism that reduces physical distance, a barrier to collaboration, enables value co-creation that drives innovation and business transformation, increases sales and networks, and provides local communities with practitioners who have enhanced knowledge and technology for use in their practices.

The suggestions to be found in these stories can assist conference organisers to provide 'out of the ordinary' social experiences and ensure they continue into the future. Ideas include:

- Know who your audience is; delegates are often highly self-directed and problem-focused.

- Consider the conference outcomes that the hosting organisation would like to achieve. This may involve setting short-term objectives and long-term legacy goals, as well as being alert to the need to adapt and be flexible.

- Welcome diverse disciplines.

- Provide engaging speakers who can deliver cutting-edge research.

- Have well thought out programs that cater to a range of needs.

- Facilitate plenty of interaction by considering how to create environments where attendees can casually speak to each other, in addition to conference dinners and informal events.

- Consider accessibility in terms of cost for early career academics and practitioners as they can gain the exposure, education and opportunities that will help them be the next generation of high achievers.

- Create opportunities for the conference to be connected with and communicated to the wider public sphere: involve the use of media personalities; generate interest so that people ask questions; welcome the general public; capture public sentiment before and after the conference; connect delegates with government and industry.

These insights and tips can inform a conference business model that seeks to value conferences and assists in realising their full potential, at the same time acknowledging their power as transformative social network spaces.

Conceptualising An Expanded Business Model For Conferences

Business models are useful for capturing, mapping and understanding the full value of entities (Osterwalder, Pigneur & Tucci 2005). Conferences are entities that are not always fully appreciated or understood by their many stakeholders. Therefore, we believe that conceptualising a business model of conferences is a useful exercise to take into account the complexity shown in Table 1. Boons and Lüdeke-Freund (2013) argue that business models support the strategic marketing of innovative processes, products and services, and can be adapted to provide competitive advantage. Through an extensive literature review they identified three broad streams of business models: organisational business models used as a strategic management tool to improve a company's value chain; technological business models that focus on the consequences of particular technologies in terms of how firms organise to earn profits; and strategy-oriented business models that create and deliver customer value (Boons & Lüdeke-Freund 2013, p. 10). From this review they argue that a generic business model incorporates four elements:

- Value offering: the value offered to customers by means of goods and services

- Supply chain: the business infrastructure, and the structure and management of supplier relationships

- Consumer interface: the structure and management of customer relationships

- Financial model: the costs and benefits from the above three elements and their distribution to stakeholders in the firm.

The stories in this book and our previous research suggest that the application of a business model to conferences may look something like Figure 2. We have drawn on the findings of Boons and Lüdeke-Freund (2013) to develop this conference business model. The four elements are elaborated below.

DIAGRAM 2 CONFERENCE BUSINESS MODEL (CBM)

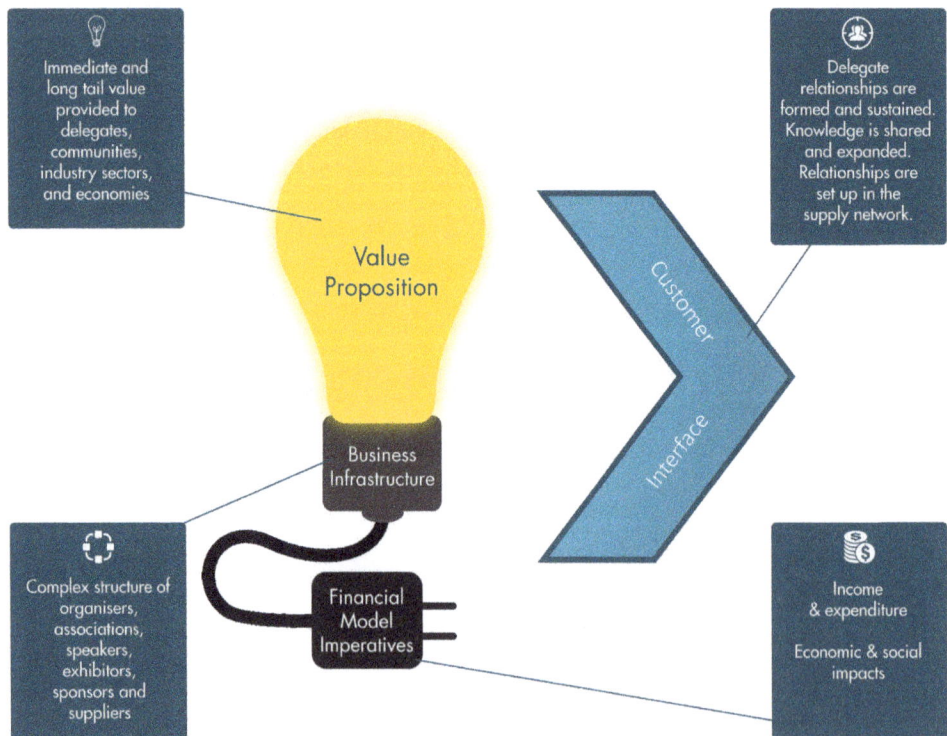

The value proposition gives an overall view of a company's bundle of products and services that provide measurable social value in concert with economic value (Osterwalder et al. 2005). In the context of conferences, the traditional value measure of tourism contribution is the tip of the value proposition iceberg. The bulk of the value is offered by means of knowledge and networking opportunities via sessions, plenaries, workshops, trade exhibitions, various intellectual activities and a social program which leads to immediate and long tail outcomes of wider societal and economic benefit. The value proposition is facilitated through dialogue that occurs temporally and spatially throughout the course of the event. During and after the conference the production and consumption of value continues among participants and an associated network of actors.

Business infrastructure dictates how the activities and resources of the conference are structured and managed. It represents a complex network of suppliers, service providers and other supporting units that perform the functions vital for producing the tangible and intangible services that support the core activities required by conference attendees (Baltacioglu et al. 2007). 'Business infrastructure portrays the network of cooperative agreements with other companies necessary to efficiently offer value' (Osterwalder et al. 2005, p. 18). These may include IT support, food and beverage suppliers, venue operator, exhibitors and sponsors.

The customer interface is twofold: (1) It reflects the attendee's ability to take responsibility for their consumption and distribution of knowledge and practices pre-, during and post-conference; (2) It describes the various means of the conference to connect with attendees and explains how a conference establishes links between itself and its different attendee segments – academics, practitioners, organisers, associations, exhibitors, sponsors.

The financial model reflects an appropriate distribution of economic costs and benefits among actors involved in the business model and also accounts for the conference's economic and social impacts (Maas & Boons 2010). The financial model describes the revenue flows for venues, suppliers, sponsors, exhibitors and attendees.

Given the many different types of conferences staged globally, the CBM has been presented somewhat generically to allow for empirical refinement. Theoretically, the CBM provides a basic set of principles which need to be fulfilled in order to facilitate a successful conference that generates both short-term and long-term societal and economic benefits. At the heart of the CBM is knowing that physical co-presence is important for having powerful and complex forms of interaction in which both language and nonverbal communication is involved. This enables the unique establishment of common reference frames and moments of serendipity that drive innovation and social change.

The CBM's practical contribution lies in the creation of concepts and tools that can help managers to capture value, communicate objectives to stakeholders, design for legacy, and react to competitors to improve existing conference outcomes. We encourage others to build on this work to advance the development of the CBM.

Further Research

The case studies in this book demonstrate the long tail value of conferences for delegates and their professions, communities and the wider economy. For a country like Australia, where geographic isolation has the potential to impede global collaboration and diffusion of knowledge, conferences provide an opportunity to transcend such difficulties.

Scientific collaboration emanates from the structure of social relations among knowledge producers. Successful research projects translate into new resources facilitating social actions such as the generation of knowledge through presentation at conferences and journal publication, or the attainment of specified objectives (Ynalvez & Shrum 2011, p. 206).

However, there are still many questions to be answered and further research is needed. For example, can we be sure that the outcomes of conferences are always positive? Should we consider the value in outcomes of conferences in terms of a continuum – at one end the rewards may be highly energising, engaging and long lasting, whilst at the other end relatively little may be gained?

Do the stories in this book suggest contextual similarities? If so, would further categorisation be useful? For example, would there be a difference in the scale of benefits between small and large conferences or different types of conferences?

Have the stories adequately represented a long tail understanding of conference benefits (practical, theoretical)? Are these stories biased towards the maintenance of individual or stakeholder interests? How can the less tangible elements of conferences be elucidated, and is there a need for tangible measurement (i.e. if it is not measured, it does not count)?

How can conferences do more to assist researchers and practitioners to resolve the scientific and social dilemmas they face? How can conferences be informed by the dilemmas that practitioners have to resolve? Will technology, and especially social media, reshape how networks are formed and sustained? Will technology eventually change the way conferences operate? If so, how can the crucial face-to-face element be retained? Can venue design play a stronger role in the creation of social spaces? Has the CBM fully captured the value of conferences?

Although the stories in this book are based on a small number of case studies, they provide clear evidence of the long tail of conferences.
They show that through a meeting of minds, networks and friendships, serendipitous discoveries occur which lead to many benefits for society. We hope that readers are as inspired as we were. The stories show that 'powers for change lie in the hands of those who have the imagination and insight to see that the new invention has offered them new liberties of action, that old constraints have been removed, that their political will, or their sheer greed are no longer frustrated; and that they can act in new ways' (Cherry 1977, p. 112). The remarkable individuals, discoveries and contributions within this book will stay with us for many years to come. They pay homage also to the many other stories emanating from conferences that will inspire and delight us long into the future.

Select Bibliography

Key Texts

Anderson, C. (2004). The Long Tail Wired. Retrieved August 15, 2016, from http://www.wired.com/2004/10/tail/ or http://www.longtail.com/about.html

Bahlmann, M. D., Huysman, M. H., Elfring, T., & Groenewegen, P. (2009). Global pipelines or global buzz?: a micro-level approach towards the knowledge-based view of clusters. *Research Memorandum*, 2, 1–32.

Baltacioglu, T., Ada, E., Kaplan, M.D., Yurt, O. & Kaplan, Y.C. (2007). A new framework for service supply chains. *Service Industry Journal*, 27, 105–124. https://doi.org/10.1080/02642060601122629

Bassett, L. E. (1933). Why conventions? *Quarterly Journal of Speech*, 19(4), 561–566. https://doi.org/10.1080/00335633309379985

Bathelt, H., Malmberg, A., & Maskell, P. (2004). Clusters and knowledge: local buzz, global pipelines and the process of knowledge creation. *Progress in human geography*, 28(1), 31–56. https://doi.org/10.1191/0309132504ph469oa

Bingham, A., & Spradlin, D. (2011). *The Long Tail of Expertise*. Upper Saddle River: Pearson Education.

Brown, G. W., & Tukey, J. W. (1946). Some distributions of sample means. *The Annals of Mathematical Statistics*, 17(1), 1–12. https://doi.org/10.1214/aoms/1177731017

Brynjolfsson, E., Hu, Y., & Simester, D. (2011). Goodbye pareto principle, hello long tail: the effect of search costs on the concentration of product sales. *Management Science*, 57(8), 1373–1386. https://doi.org/10.1287/mnsc.1110.1371

Brynjolfsson, E., Hu, Y. J., & Smith, M. D. (2006). From niches to riches: Anatomy of the long tail. *Sloan Management Review*, 47(4), 67–71.

Brynjolfsson, E., Hu, Y. J., & Smith, M. D. (2010). The longer tail: The changing shape of Amazon's sales distribution curve. https://doi.org/10.2139/ssrn.1679991

Business Events Council of Australia. (2009). Business Events Summit – Post Summit Report. Retrieved October 25, 2016, from http://www.businesseventscouncil.org.au/files/be_summit_09_final_report.pdf

Business Events Council of Australia. (2010). Business Events Council of Australia (BECA) Pre-Budget Submission to Federal Government 2010–11. Retrieved September 26, 2017, from http://www.businesseventscouncil.org.au/files/BECA_PBS_2011.pdf

Business Events Sydney. (2009). Congress Outcomes. Sydney: Burson Marsteller.

Business Events Sydney. (2016a). Associations. Retrieved October 27, 2016, from http://www.businesseventssydney.com.au

Business Events Sydney. (2016b). Interview with Michael Boyer. Retrieved November 9, 2016, from https://businesseventssydney.com.au/about-us/our-events/previous-events/besydney-ambassador-dinner-and-investiture-2016/

Carlsen, J. (1995). Gathering information: meetings and conventions sector research in Australia. *Journal of Tourism Studies*, 6(2), 21.

Carlsen, J., Getz, D., & Soutar, G. (2000). Event evaluation research. *Event Management*, 6(4), 247–257. https://doi.org/10.3727/152599500108751408

Cherry, C. (1977). The telephone system: creator of mobility and social change. In D. S. Pool I (Ed.), *The social impact of the telephone* (pp. 112–126). Cambridge: MIT Press.

Dwyer, L., Mellor, R., Mistilis, N., & Mules, T. (2000). A framework for assessing "tangible" and "intangible" impacts of events and conventions. *Event Management*, 6(3), 175–189.

Edwards, D. C., Foley, C. T., & Schlenker, K. (2011). Beyond Tourism Benefits: Measuring the Social Legacies of Business Events, Report prepared for Business Events Sydney. Sydney: University of Technology Sydney.

Foley, C. (2017). The art of wasting time: sociability, friendship, community and holidays. *Leisure Studies*, 36(1), 1–20. https://doi.org/10.1080/02614367.2015.1055296

Foley, C., Edwards, D., & Schlenker, K. (2014). Business events and friendship: Leveraging the sociable legacies. *Event Management*, 18(1), 53–64. https://doi.org/10.3727/152599514X13883555341887

Foley, C., Schlenker, K., Edwards, D., & Lewis-Smith, L. (2013). Determining business event legacies beyond the tourism spend: An Australian case study approach. *Event Management*, 17(3), 311–322. https://doi.org/10.3727/15259951 3X13708863378079

Foley, C. T., Edwards, D., & Hergesell, A. (2016). Conferences: catalysts for thriving economies. Sydney: University of Technology Sydney.

Foley, C. T., Edwards, D., Hergesell, A., & Schlenker, K. (2014). Asian incentive events in New South Wales: Expenditure and Retail Impact. Sydney: University of Technology Sydney.

Foley, C. T., Edwards, D., Hergesell, A., & Schlenker, K. (2014). Estimating inscope expenditure attributed to business events in New South Wales. Sydney: University of Technology Sydney.

Foley, C. T., Edwards, D., & Schlenker, K. (2014). Beyond Tourism Benefits: building an international profile. Report prepared for Future Convention Cities Initiative (FCCI). Sydney: University of Technology Sydney.

Foley, C. T., Schlenker, K., & Edwards, D. C. (2010). A Scoping Study of Business Events: Beyond Tourism Benefits. Sydney: University of Technology Sydney.

Hickson, I., Mark. (2006). Raising the Question# 4 Why Bother Attending Conferences? *Communication Education*, 55(4), 464–468. https://doi. org/10.1080/03634520600917632

Jago, L., & Deery, M. (2010). Delivering innovation, knowledge and performance: the role of business events. Retrieved June 21, 2017, from http://www. businesseventscouncil.org.au/files/Business_Events_Innovation_Report_Mar10. pdf

Joint Meetings Industry Council. (2008). Understanding the Value of the Meetings Industry. Retrieved September 26, 2017, from http://www.themeetingsindustry.org/ storage/perspective_articles/Article_Understanding_the_Value_08.10.pdf

Maas, K. E. H., & Boons, F. A. A. (2010). CSR as a strategic activity: value creation, redistribution and integration. In: Louche, C., Idowu, S., Leal Filho, W. (Eds.), *Innovative CSR: From Risk Management to Value Creation*. London: Greenleaf, pp. 154–172. https://doi.org/10.9774/GLEAF.978-1-907643-26-2_9

McDonald, M., Wearing, S., & Ponting, J. (2007). Narcissism and neo-liberalism: Work, leisure, and alienation in an era of consumption. *Loisir et Société/Society and Leisure*, 30(2), 489–510. https://doi.org/10.1080/07053436.2007.10707762

Osterwalder, A., Pigneur, Y., & Tucci, C. L. (2005). Clarifying business models: Origins, present, and future of the concept. *Communications of the Association for Information Systems*, 16(1), 1.

Pickernell, D., O'Sullivan, D., Senyard, J. M., & Keast, R. L. (2007). Social capital and network building for enterprise in rural areas: can festivals and special events contribute. Paper presented at the 30th Institute for Small Business and Entrepreneurship Conference, Glasgow.

Pittman, J., & McLaughlin, B. (2012). Professional Conferences, Social Capital and Tourism: Is the Alliance in Jeopardy. *Tourism and Hospitality*, 1(2), 1–3. https://doi.org/10.4172/2167-0269.1000e109

Roberts, R. M. (1989). *Serendipity: Accidental discoveries in science*. Canada: Wiley.

Small, J., Harris, C., Wilson, E., & Ateljevic, I. (2011). Voices of women: A memory-work reflection on work-life dis/harmony in tourism academia. *Journal of Hospitality, Leisure, Sports and Tourism Education* (Pre-2012), 10(1), 23. https://doi.org/10.3794/johlste.101.265

Teulan, B. (2010). Conferences Driving Innovation, Knowledge and Investment, Miles Clarke Business Events Communication Award Winner. Retrieved June 21, 2017, from http://www.businesseventscouncil.org.au/

The Business Events Industry Strategy Group. (2008). National Business Events Strategy for Australia 2020: the business of events – Australia's untapped potential. Retrieved June 21, 2017, from http://www.businesseventscouncil.org.au/files/bes_ex_summary_nov08.pdf

Vargo, S. L., & Lusch, R. F. (2011). It's all B2B... and beyond: Toward a systems perspective of the market. *Industrial marketing management*, 40(2), 181–187. https://doi.org/10.1016/j.indmarman.2010.06.026

Von Hippel, E. (2005). *Democratizing Innovation*. Cambridge: MIT Press.

Wood, E. H. (2008). An impact evaluation framework: Local government community festivals. *Event Management*, 12(3-4), 171–185. https://doi.org/10.3727/152599509789659768

Ynalvez, M. A., & Shrum, W. M. (2011). Professional networks, scientific collaboration, and publication productivity in resource-constrained research institutions in a developing country. *Research Policy*, 40(2), 204–216. https://doi.org/10.1016/j.respol.2010.10.004

Zhu, X., Song, B., Ni, Y., Ren, Y., & Li, R. (2016). Prosumer Economy—From Supply Chain to Prosumer Economy in *Business Trends in the Digital Era: Evolution of Theories and Applications* (pp. 123–141). Singapore: Springer Singapore.

Ziman, J. (2002). *Real science: What it is and what it means*. Cape Town: Cambridge University Press.

Interviews

Altman, L. (2009). A. Stone Freedberg, Pioneer in Study of Ulcers, Dies at 101. Retrieved June 23, 2017, from http://www.nytimes.com/2009/08/24/health/24freedberg.htm

American Institute of Physics. (2007). Brian Schmidt – Session I. Retrieved June 23, 2017, from https://www.aip.org/history-programs/niels-bohr-library/oral-histories/33746-1

Australasia Extracellular Vesicles Conference. (2017). A/Prof Mary Bebawy. Retrieved June 20, 2017, from http://www.australasia-ev.org/invited-speakers/show/560

Australia's Chief Scientist. (2015). KEYNOTE ADDRESS to the National Press Club for Science Meets Parliament. Retrieved June 23, 2017, from http://www.chiefscientist.gov.au/2015/03/keynote-address-to-the-national-press-club-for-science-meets-parliament-2/

Australia Academy of Science. (2017). Professor Ian Frazer, immunologist. Retrieved June 21, 2017, from https://www.science.org.au/learning/general-audience/history/interviews-australian-scientists/professor-ian-frazer-immunologist

Australian Cancer Research Foundation. (2017). Bio-Professor Ian Frazer. Retrieved June 21, 2017, from https://acrf.com.au/about-australian-cancer-research-foundation/medical-research-advisory-committee/professor-ian-frazer/

Australian Infectious Diseases. (2017). Professor Ian Frazer. Retrieved June 21, 2017, from http://www.aidrc.org.au/ian-frazer

Australian Museum. (n.d.). INDIGENOUS AUSTRALIANS OVERVIEW. Retrieved June 23, 2017, from https://australianmuseum.net.au/indigenous-australia

Australian Women's Archives Project. (2006). Putting Skirts on the Sacred Benches: Women Candidates for the New South Wales Parliament. Retrieved June 23, 2017, from http://www.womenaustralia.info/exhib/pssb/home.html

Bowtell, B. (n.d.). APPLYING THE PARADOX OF PREVENTION: ERADICATE HIV. Retrieved June 16, 2017, from https://griffithreview.com/articles/applying-the-paradox-of-prevention-eradicate-hiv/

Brown, D. (2012). Everything's different (almost) since last international AIDS conference in U.S. Retrieved June 23, 2017, from https://www.washingtonpost.com/national/health-science/everythings-different-almost-since-last-international-aids-conference-in-us/2012/07/21/gJQA5pXr0W_story.html?utm_term=.fa2e4d23c511

Burney, L. (1999). Keynote address: Finding the Ground Rules. In R. Craven (Ed.), *Education for the future: Collected papers of the 9th annual Aboriginal Studies Assocation Conference* (pp. 26–28). Leichardt, NSW: Aboriginal Studies Association.

Burney, L. (2000). Not just a challenge, an opportunity. In M. Grattan (Ed.), *Reconciliation: essays on Australian reconciliation* (pp. 65–73). Melbourne: Bookman Press.

Callaghan, R., Luk, F., & Bebawy, M. (2014). Inhibition of the multidrug resistance P-glycoprotein: time for a change of strategy? *Drug Metabolism and Disposition*, 42(4), 623–631. https://doi.org/10.1124/dmd.113.056176

Criterion Conferences. (2016). Paying Tribute to Outgoing Chief Scientist Professor Ian Chubb. Retrieved June 23, 2017, from https://www.criterionconferences.com/blog/government/paying-tribute-outgoing-chief-scientist-professor-ian-chubb/

D'Souza, C. (2003). Linda Burney: an interview. *Indigenous Law Bulletin*, 5(26), 8–9.

Dean, T. (2012). Brian Schmidt: in conversation. Retrieved June 23, 2017, from https://theconversation.com/brian-schmidt-in-conversation-8383

Dingle, S. (2014). Neal Blewett and Peter Baume honoured for bipartisan work against AIDS epidemic of 1980s. Retrieved June 23, 2017, from http://www.abc.net.au/news/2014-07-16/poltical-rivals-honoured-for-joint-aids-work/5598392

Energy Matters. (2015). Solar Pioneer Wins Australian Academy of Science Award. Retrieved June 21, 2017, from http://www.energymatters.com.au/renewable-news/green-award-solar-em5209/

Food and Agriculture Organization of the United Nations. (2014). The State of World Fisheries and Aquaculture. Rome: Food and Agriculture Organization of the United Nations.

Food Matters. (2017). Seaweed Superfoods. Retrieved June 23, 2017, from http://www.foodmatters.com/superfoods/seaweed-superfoods

Ford, I. (2013). Blind-siding cancer. Retrieved June 23, 2017, from http://d7.newsroom.uts.edu.au.tmp.anchor.net.au/news/2013/07/blind-siding-cancer

Fuss, E. (2015). Could seaweed farming be Australia's next aquaculture industry? Retrieved June 23, 2017, from http://www.abc.net.au/local/stories/2014/09/21/4091941.htm

Galvin, R. (2015). Increasing Indigenous education workforce key to closing the gap. Retrieved June 23, 2017, from http://w3.unisa.edu.au/unisanews/2015/November/story14.asp

Goldie, B. (2015). Human trial begins on health benefits of seaweed fibre. Retrieved June 23, 2017, from http://media.uow.edu.au/releases/UOW204467.html

Goodyer, P. (2014). How to introduce seaweed, 'the other green superfood', into your diet. Retrieved June 23, 2017, from http://www.smh.com.au/lifestyle/diet-and-fitness/how-to-introduce-seaweed-the-other-green-superfood-into-your-diet-20141114-11mjjw.html

Hannam, P. (2015). Solar's rise as seen by a tech guru, an ex-billionaire and an emerging talent. Retrieved June 21, 2017, from http://www.smh.com.au/environment/un-climate-conference/solars-rise-as-seen-by-a-tech-guru-an-exbillionaire-and-an-emerging-talent-20150531-ghds3b.html

Haspel, T. (2015). Seaweed is easy to grow, sustainable and nutritious. But it'll never be kale. Retrieved June, 2017, from https://www.washingtonpost.com/lifestyle/food/seaweed-is-easy-to-grow-sustainable-and-nutritious-but-itll-never-be-kale/2015/10/26/1d1719b8-7750-11e5-b9c1-f03c48c96ac2_story.html?utm_term=.0ce6f97034b3

Henderson, A. (2016). Sung into her seat: Indigenous MP Linda Burney makes history as the world watches. Retrieved June 20, 2017, from http://www.abc.net.au/news/2016-09-07/indigenous-mp-makes-history-as-world-watches-wiradjuri-welcome/7822482

Hordern, T. (2012). Professor Martin Green awarded for solar research. Retrieved June 21, 2017, from http://www.ecocitizenaustralia.com.au/professor-martin-green-awarded-solar-research/

Horton, D. (Ed.). (1994). *The Encyclopaedia of Aboriginal Australia: Aboriginal and Torres Strait Islander history, society and culture*. Canberra: Aboriginal Studies Press for AIATSIS.

Indigenous Conference Services. (n.d.). 2015 INTERNATIONAL INDIGENOUS HEALTH CONFERENCE. Retrieved June 23, 2017, from https://www.indigenousconferences.com/2015-indigenous-health-conference

International AIDS society. (2014). CONFERENCE Summary Report. Retrieved June 20, 2017, from http://www.aids2014.org/webcontent/file/AIDS2014_Summary_Report_Dec2014.pdf

Jaiswal, R., Luk, F., Dalla, P. V., Grau, G. E. R., & Bebawy, M. (2013). Breast cancer-derived microparticles display tissue selectivity in the transfer of resistance proteins to cells. *PloS one*, 8(4), e61515. https://doi.org/10.1371/journal.pone.0061515

Jean-Michel Cousteau's Ocean Futures Society. (2014). The future of sustainable fish farming. Retrieved June 23, 2017, from http://www.oceanfutures.org/news/blog/future-sustainable-fish-farming

Jessica, T. (2005). Delayed Gratification: Why it Took Everybody So Long to Acknowledge that Bacteria Cause Ulcers. Retrieved June 23, 2017, from http://www.jyi.org/issue/delayed-gratification-why-it-took-everybody-so-long-to-acknowledge-that-bacteria-cause-ulcers/

Kate, L. (2016). Brian Schmidt: ANU Vice Chancellor, Nobel Laureate, cosmologist. Retrieved June 23, 2017, from http://www.theaustralian.com.au/life/weekend-australian-magazine/brian-schmidt-anu-vice-chancellor-nobel-laureate-cosmologist/news-story/418c885fd760907d72cb04d186881d58

Krubner, L. (n.d.). Sometimes peer review delays progress for many decades. Retrieved June 21, 2017, from http://www.smashcompany.com/technology/sometimes-peer-review-delays-progress-for-many-decades

Lee, J. (2016). Chief Scientist Ian Chubb's parting words: Science 'must always trump make-believe'. Retrieved June 23, 2017, from http://www.smh.com.au/federal-politics/political-news/chief-scientist-ian-chubbs-parting-words-science-must-always-trump-makebelieve-20160119-gm99bi.html

Leschin-Hoar, C. (2014). Help for Kelp – Seaweed Slashers See Harvesting Cuts Coming. Retrieved June 23, 2017, from https://www.scientificamerican.com/article/help-for-kelp-seaweed-slashers-see-harvesting-cuts-coming/

Lu, J. F., Pokharel, D., & Bebawy, M. (2015). MRP1 and its role in anticancer drug resistance. *Drug metabolism reviews*, 47(4), 406–419. https://doi.org/10.3109/03602532.2015.1105253

Marshall, B. (2002). *Helicobacter pioneers: firsthand accounts from the scientists who discovered helicobacters 1892–1982*. Oxford: Wiley-Blackwell.

Marshall, B., & Adams, P. C. (2008). Helicobacter pylori: A Nobel pursuit? *Canadian Journal of Gastroenterology and Hepatology*, 22(11), 895–896. https://doi.org/10.1155/2008/459810

Maskell, P., Bathelt, H., & Malmberg, A. (2005). Building global knowledge pipelines: The role of temporary clusters. DRUID Working Paper No. 05–20. Danish Research Unit for Industrial Dynamics.

Moss, E. (2017). Ten years on, Professor Ian Frazer recalls 'lucky' discovery of cervical cancer vaccine. Retrieved June 23, 2017, from http://www.abc.net.au/news/2017-03-25/ian-frazer-recalls-lucky-discovery-of-cervical-cancer-vaccine/8385872

NASA. (2001). A Supernova Sheds Light on Dark Energy. Retrieved June 23, 2017, from https://science.nasa.gov/science-news/science-at-nasa/2001/ast03apr_1/

NASA. (2013). What is a Supernova? Retrieved June 23, 2017, from https://www.nasa.gov/audience/forstudents/5-8/features/nasa-knows/what-is-a-supernova.html

National Health and Medical Research Council. (2009). A conversation with Professor Barry Marshall. Retrieved June 23, 2017, from https://www.nhmrc.gov.au/media/podcasts/2009/conversation-professor-barry-marshall

Newton, J. (2014). Academic Pia Winberg, chefs Mark Best and Victor Liong and others are planting seaweed on menus. Retrieved June 23, 2017, from http://www.theaustralian.com.au/archive/executive-living/academic-pia-winberg-chefs-mark-best-and-victor-liong-and-others-are-planting-seaweed-on-menus/news-story/51a5e0e238ba264096c8eac9a31477f8

Niall. (2011). Measuring the Universe from start to finish. Retrieved June 23, 2017, from http://stories.scienceinpublic.com.au/stories-of-astronomy-2012/measuring-the-universe/

Ocean Harvest Technology. (2013). Tide must turn to use potential of seaweed. Retrieved June 23, 2017, from http://oceanharvest.ie/tide-must-turn-to-use-potential-of-seaweed/

Parliament of Australia. (n.d.). Hon Linda Burney MP. Retrieved June 21, 2017, from http://www.aph.gov.au/Senators_and_Members/Parliamentarian?MPID=8GH

Paul, N. (2016). Seaweed aquaculture: an innovation platform for the Blue Economy. Retrieved June 23, 2017, from http://theblueeconomychallenge.com/seaweed-aquaculture-in-the-tropics-an-innovation-platform-for-the-blue-economy/

Phillips, N. (2014). Nobel laureate Brian Schmidt fires broadside at Australia's research strategy. Retrieved June 23, 2017, from http://www.smh.com.au/national/nobel-laureate-brian-schmidt-fires-broadside-at-australias-research-strategy-20140723-zw0ru.html

Phys.org. (2015). Revealed: Helicobacter pylori's secret weapon. Retrieved June 22, 2017, from https://phys.org/news/2015-08-revealed-helicobacter-pylori-secret-weapon.html

Respect Learn Health. (n.d.). Linda Burney Biography. Retrieved June 23, 2017, from http://www.nrlcommunity.com.au/indigenous/arl_indigenous_council/linda_burney.html

Rjvanderbei. (2011). Nobel Prize in Physics 2011 – The Accelerating Universe. Retrieved June 23, 2017, from http://voices.nationalgeographic.com/2011/10/12/nobel-prize-in-physics-2011/

Schmidt, B. (2017). Brian Schmidt: why funding science infrastructure is essential. Retrieved June 23, 2017, from https://theconversation.com/brian-schmidt-why-funding-science-infrastructure-is-essential-38303

Schmidt, L. (2011). Profile: Ian Chubb. Retrieved June 23, 2017, from http://www.smh.com.au/money/investing/profile-ian-chubb-20110613-1g0sh.html

Seafood Source. (November 23, 2015). Seaweed: fleeting trend or realistic future food. Retrieved September 26, 2017, from https://www.seafoodsource.com/commentary/seaweed-fleeting-trend-or-realistic-future-food

Smart, J., & Swain, S. (Eds.). (2014). 'Burney, Linda Jean', *The Encyclopedia of Women and Leadership in Twentieth-Century Australia*, Australian Women's Archives Project.

Smith, E. (2017). A bug's life: *H. pylori* and stomach cancer. Retrieved June 20, 2017, from http://scienceblog.cancerresearchuk.org/2014/03/07/a-bugs-life-h-pylori-and-stomach-cancer/

Suzuki, H., Warren, R., & Marshall, B. (2016). Helicobacter pylori. Tokyo: Springer. https://doi.org/10.1007/978-4-431-55705-0

Swan, N. (2008). Professor Barry Marshall, gastroenterologist. Retrieved 2017, from https://www.science.org.au/learning/general-audience/history/interviews-australian-scientists/professor-barry-marshall

Tarantola, A. (2014). From Ice Cream to Toothpaste: Seaweed's Hidden Uses. Retrieved June 23, 2017, from https://www.gizmodo.com.au/2014/10/seaweed-the-incredible-edible-algae-we-use-for-way-more-than-sushi/

Trove National Library of Australia. (2009). Burney, Linda Jean (1957-). Retrieved June 23, 2017, from http://nla.gov.au/nla.party-723086

UTS. (n.d.). Associate Professor Mary Bebawy. Retrieved June 23, 2017, from http://www.uts.edu.au/staff/mary.bebawy

Venue Shell System. (n.d.). Australia's cleanest, greenest marine biotechnology business. Retrieved June 23, 2017, from https://www.venusshellsystems.com.au/about-us/

Williams, R. (2013). Solar Superman. Retrieved June 21, 2017, from http://www.australiaunlimited.com/science/solar-superman

Winberg, P. (2008). Using Algae in the 21st Century. Barton: Rural Industries Research and Development Corporation.

Winberg, P. (2012). Sustainable marine food production systems-the case for seaweed. *Australasian Medical Journal*, 5(12).

World Science Festival. (2015). To Infinity and Beyond: The Accelerating Universe. Retrieved June 23, 2017, from https://www.youtube.com/watch?v=pcKdA2-W0X0#t=17.584248

Yeoman, R. (n.d.). Dished up: rediscovering seaweed links in food chain. Retrieved June 23, 2017, from http://frdc.com.au/knowledge/publications/fish/Pages/22-1_articles/20-dished-up-rediscovering-seaweed.aspx

About the Authors

Deborah Edwards is an Associate Professor in the Business School, University of Technology Sydney. She is a Research Associate of the Australian Centre for Event Management (ACEM). With a wide interest in a variety of areas including business events, visitor experiences and tourism sustainability, she has published extensively. Her previous collaborative books include Innovation Networks for Sustainable Tourism: Case studies and cross-case analysis (2012), Understanding the Sustainable Development of Tourism (2010), City Spaces – Tourist Places: Urban Tourism Precincts (2008), and Innovation for Sustainable Tourism: International Case Studies (2008). Her industry experience underpins her philosophy as a researcher and she views industry liaison as integral to delivering applied research that assists industry to meet desired objectives.

Carmel Foley is a Research Associate of the Australian Centre for Event Management (ACEM) and the director of event management programs at the University of Technology Sydney where she is an Associate Professor in the Business School. Carmel's research projects have included triple bottom line event evaluation for the Sustainable Tourism Cooperative Research Centre, evaluation of the Parkes Elvis Festival for Parkes Shire Council, the series of Beyond Tourism Benefits studies for Business Events Sydney, economic and social value of live music venues for Sydney Entertainment Centre, expenditure studies for Business Events Sydney, and conference legacy projects for Seoul Convention Bureau, Tourism Toronto and Durban KwaZulu-Natal. Carmel Foley and Deborah Edwards are currently working on an international project with the Joint Meetings Industry Council to redefine the value proposition of the global business events industry.

Cheryl Malone is an award-winning professional writer and communicator and the founder of Wordswotwork where she specialises in corporate histories, life stories, funding and award submissions, mass communication and marketing. She has taught at both University of Technology Sydney and Griffith University in the areas of journalism, public writing, events, sport and tourism.